Political Economy of
Public Education Finance

Political Economy of Public Education Finance

Equity, Political Institutions, and Inter-School District Competition

Nandan K. Jha

LEXINGTON BOOKS

Lanham • Boulder • New York • London

Published by Lexington Books
An imprint of The Rowman & Littlefield Publishing Group, Inc.
4501 Forbes Boulevard, Suite 200, Lanham, Maryland 20706
www.rowman.com

6 Tinworth Street, London SE11 5AL, United Kingdom

British Library Cataloguing in Publication Information Available

Library of Congress Cataloging-in-Publication Data Available

Names: Jha, Nandan K., author.
Title: Political economy of public education finance : equity, political institutions, and inter-school district competition / Nandan K. Jha.
Description: Lanham, Maryland : Lexington Books, 2020. | Includes bibliographical references and index. | Summary: "Political Economy of Public Education Finance clarifies organizational, political, and socioeconomic contexts in equity in public education spending, arguing that through appropriate policy and reorganization of school finance, policymakers can reform the organizational and political set-up of school districts for more effective public education"— Provided by publisher.
Identifiers: LCCN 2020002927 (print) | LCCN 2020002928 (ebook) |
    ISBN 9781498590709 (cloth) | ISBN 9781498590716 (epub)
    ISBN 9781498590723 (pbk)
Subjects: LCSH: Education—United States—Finance. | Public schools—United States—Finance | School choice—Political aspects—United States. | School districts—United States—Administration
Classification: LCC LB2825 J53 2020 (print) | LCC LB2825 (ebook) |
    DDC 379.1/1—dc23
LC record available at https://lccn.loc.gov/2020002927
LC ebook record available at https://lccn.loc.gov/2020002928

Contents

List of Figures and Tables

FIGURES

TABLES

Introduction

Political Economy of Public Education Finance: Equity, Political Institutions, and Inter-School District Competition

INTRODUCTION, OVERVIEW, AND STUDY SIGNIFICANCE

Equity in school district spending is of paramount importance in the literature on K-12 public education in the United States. This study takes a comprehensive examination of the intersection between local political institutions and school choice and how this intersection influences funding disparities across urban school districts in the United States. This study presents a systematic analysis of several pertinent issues in the context of the urban K-12 public education finance in the United States including a thorough examination of inequities, a ubiquitous dimension of school choice, and types and roles of local political institutions.

Public schools enroll about 90 percent of students in the United States. The fiscal burden of public education in the United States is shared between local, state, and federal governments. Currently, about 50 percent of funding comes from state governments, 40 percent comes from the local government, and about 9 percent comes from the federal government. There is a lot of variation in per-pupil funding across school districts in the United States, both between and within states. The rich suburban districts spend more money than poor urban school districts because the former enjoy higher per-pupil property wealth. Rich districts can raise more revenue at a lower tax rate, whereas a poor district cannot raise enough revenue even with higher property tax rate. This double disadvantage is a major roadblock in according equitable and adequate educational opportunities and equal protection to child. The poor urban school districts also house disproportionately high proportions of minority and other disadvantaged and difficult-to-teach students.

1

This sorting of students in school districts with varying per-pupil funding in the urban regional education market also reflects a ubiquitous form of school choice: the competition among public school districts as providers of public education for attracting different segments of students. The school districts have relied on some form of zoning at the local level. Parents when making decision to choose their residences also choose by default their child's school. This has resulted in sorting of parents in rich and poor school districts. Since at least the early 1970s, federal and state governments in the United States have tried to level the field, but with only a limited success. This marginal success in terms of funding equity across school districts has come about on two fronts. One, state governments have stepped up their share in the pie. Two, state supreme courts have ordered their respective governments to make funding system more equitable. This study covers these two aspects in the following chapters.

These providers of public education are in turn managed by different types of political institutions at the district level. In according equitable public education to students within their respective jurisdictions, these political institutions must take into account the level of interjurisdictional competition in the urban regional market context. Therefore, these two factors intersect significantly in determining the level of per-pupil funding across school districts. However, the research on the effects of school choice (operationalized as interschool district competition) and local political institutions on unequal school district spending is not adequate. Existing literature has neither studied the joint effects of school choice and local political institutions on school district funding nor their effects with regard to equity. Both understanding equity dimension of school district funding and moving incrementally toward a more equitable public education in the United States are important concerns in popular policy debates. This book informs this debate in several critical ways. It fills key gaps in the literature by (1) developing a framework through integration of the literature on the Public Choice, the Leviathan, the Consolidated Local Government, and the Reformism models that examines the interactive roles of local political institutions and school choice on equity in spending in public schools in metropolitan areas; (2) modeling the equity effects of school choice and political institutions on school district spending; and (3) utilizing fixed effects and instrumental variable fixed effects regression models on a uniquely compiled longitudinal dataset from several sources, including the Popularly Elected Officials Survey from the US Census Bureau, the Local Education Agency (School District) Longitudinal Finance Survey, and the School District Demographics System from the National Center for Education Statistics.

Discussed in detail in chapter 8 of the book, results from fixed-effects models lend support for interactive effects of political institutions and interschool district competition on school district spending. Additive and interactive models do not robustly support the equity effects of interschool district competition on school district spending. However, results from fixed effects and instrumental variable fixed effects models support the equity effects of political institutions on school district spending in some cases. School districts with more professional political institutions are also more equitable in public education spending. These findings assume significance as they inform the policymakers in regard to why and how organizational and political contexts matter in bringing desirable educational outcomes. The policymakers can bring organizational and political changes in school districts for achieving the goal of more effective public education.

The contents of the book are substantively organized in six chapters. The book begins by laying the foundation of the subject matter in this introductory chapter. The next several chapters trace the origins of the debate on equity in education finance in school districts and chronicle policy response from government agencies and persisting disparity. This is followed by an examination of the role of equity and adequacy lawsuits in bridging some of the funding gaps. Subsequently, a ubiquitous dimension of school choice is examined for its role in explaining funding disparities across school districts. The book then investigates the different types and roles of political institutions in education finance. The book also provides a theoretical consideration of how school choice and political institutions affect funding inequity. This is followed by an empirical examination of effects of school choice and political institutions on funding inequity. The book concludes by listing significant findings, limitations, and future directions for research.

OVERVIEW

Governments are responsible for providing collective goods and services and fiscal policy is mainly concerned with raising money to pay for the cost of public programs that deliver these collective goods and services (Kraft and Furlong 2010; Lowry 2008). In the United States, there is a three-tier government system for providing public goods: federal, state, and local governments. Local governments provide a range of collective goods and services. In fact, local school districts provide K-12 public education to approximately 90% of students in the United States (Levin 2008). Furthermore, although the United States is one of the highest spenders on public education both in terms of real per-pupil dollars and as a proportion of GDP, the relative international ranking of the United States in student learning falls below the median (Hanushek and Lindseth 2009). This outcome suggests that the K-12 public education in the United States is comparatively inefficient.

This book focuses on the roles of school choice and political institutions on equity in school district spending. There is limited research on the role of school choice, defined as interschool district competition, on unequal school district spending. The few studies on the effects of interschool district competition on school district spending offer inconclusive empirical evidence (Hoxby 2000; Rothstein 2007). Furthermore, existing research has ignored the role of local political institutions. This empirical investigation will offer theoretical insights and inform the larger policy debate on the roles of school choice and political institutions in equity in school district spending and student achievement.

EQUITY IN PUBLIC EDUCATION

I investigate educational effectiveness through equity, although there are several ways to approach and study educational effectiveness (Odden and Picus 2013). Equity is distinct from other outcomes as it focuses on the variability in inputs and outcomes, without a necessary linkage between the two. In this book, equity is operationalized in terms of regional equity/inequity in school district spending, assessing whether spending varies based on within-state groupings of school districts' median household incomes. Therefore, consistent with Harris et al. (2001) and Hoxby (1996a), equity is defined as the distribution of school district spending and student achievement across school districts based on within-state groupings of school districts' median household incomes.

OVERVIEW OF THE LITERATURE, CRITICAL GAPS, AND STUDY SIGNIFICANCE

Several scholars have suggested that the educational outcomes in the United States are not commensurate with the levels of financial resources put into the public education system. In the last fifty years, spending on public schools has tripled in real terms (Peterson 2010, p. 131), and it has grown five folds in real dollars over the last century (Godwin and Kemerer 2002). Educational outcomes along racial and socioeconomic status have not kept pace with rising funding levels and with various school reforms. These policy problems also appear to be resistant to school choice, standards, and accountability-based reforms developed over the last two decades. In contextualizing these problems and proposing policy-relevant solutions, researchers have taken different positions on the questions of equity and efficiency in public education.

The literature on school choice includes studies on a range of choice and competition options including homeschooling, private schools, magnet schools, vouchers, charters, and existence of multiple school districts in a metropolitan area. School choice in the form of market-type competition can take both intra-district and interdistrict dimensions. For example, alternative forms of schools including charter schools, magnet schools, vouchers, and private schools create competitive market conditions for traditional public schools within a school district.

While there are several studies on school choice, operationalized through the presence of private schools, charter schools, and vouchers, researchers have not adequately studied school choice in the form of interschool district competition (Belfield and Levin 2005b; Gill and Booker 2015). The existence of more school districts within a metropolitan area is one dimension of school choice, as school districts compete for students. The few studies on the role of interschool district competition in school district spending narrowly focus on propositions of a single theoretical tradition of public choice pioneered by Tiebout (1956) and further developed by Ostrom et al. (1961) (Hoxby 2000; Marlow 1997, 2000; Zanzig 1997). The proponents of this market-type competition argue that having more school districts to compete for students in a metropolitan area is mutually beneficial for these school districts.

This argument parallels the general theoretical arguments about spending in local governments. Proponents of greater interlocal government competition argue for the existence of more local governments in the metropolitan area to accommodate heterogeneity in individual preferences (or public choice) for an optimal tax-expenditure bundle of public goods (Ostrom et al. 1961; Tiebout 1956). This decentralization also works against the natural tendency of local governments to extract higher taxes from residents (Craw 2008; Brennan and Buchanan 1980; Jimenez and Hendrick 2010). Existing studies ignore the theoretical propositions regarding spending advanced by the proponents of more consolidated forms of local governments. These theorists argue that greater interlocal government competition cause spillovers, urban sprawl, and racial and economic segregation. Therefore, having greater interlocal government competition in a metropolitan area is allocatively and productively inefficient (Altshuler et al. 1999; Burns 1994; DeHoog et al. 1990; Lyons and Lowery 1989; Morgan and Morescal 1999; Rusk 1993; Weiher 1991). These scholars argue that a metropolitan-wide local government is both more equitable and efficient.

This study also investigates the role of political institutions in spending and student learning, respectively. This is important because existing studies ignore the role of political institutions in the equity of school district spending. Political institutions are important to consider while investigating equity because the local political institutions influence local taxation and spending (Craw 2008; Feiock et al. 2003). Political institutions also match citizen demand with school district spending (Berkman and Plutzer 2005). Following Berkman and Plutzer (2005), Berry and Gersen (2009), and Craw (2008), this study defines and operationalizes local political institutions as electoral structures of school districts' governing boards and superintendents' offices. Additionally, school districts' autonomy in raising revenue through the imposition of property taxes is subsumed under the concept of political institutions. A limited number of studies have examined the role of local political institutions on local government spending, though not particularly in the context of school districts (Berry and Gersen 2009; Craw 2008; Mac-Donald 2008). However, researchers have not considered the effects of inter-school district competition and local political institutions together on school district spending and have ignored equity. This lack of cross-fertilization in the literature warrants a fresh investigation of the role of political institutions and interschool district competition on equity in school district spending. Furthermore, the empirical literature in the context of both public school finance and general local governments report opposing findings (see Andrews et al. 2002; Belfield and Levin 2005b; Craw 2008; Gordon and Knight 2008; Hoxby 2000; Howell-Moroney 2008; Jimenez and Hendrick 2010; Rothstein 2007). This warrants investigation and integration of additional and consistent theoretical propositions for further empirical study.

The research presented in this study is important because it clarifies why and how organizational, political, and socioeconomic contexts matter in bringing desirable educational outcomes including equity in spending. Policymakers can reform the organizational and political setup of school districts to achieve the goal of more effective public education. From a public policy perspective, findings of this research can inform the formulation of appropriate policies for better educational outcomes through reorganization of school finance.

ORGANIZATION AND GOALS

This study proceeds by developing and testing a conceptual model that combines the key propositions of multiple theoretical perspectives. This conceptual model argues that local political institutions moderate the effects of interjurisdictional competition on local government's spending. This conceptual model handles the key propositions of both the proponents of greater interjurisdictional competition and the proponents of more consolidated school districts. Chapter 5 presents the data used to test this model and empirically estimates the interactive effects of political institutions with interschool district competition on inequity in school district spending in the United States.

CONTRIBUTIONS TO THE LITERATURE

This study makes several contributions to the literature. One, the theoretical literature is extended to model the interactions of political institutions with interschool district competition in influencing equity in spending. Two, for addressing endogeneity of interschool district competition, instrumental variable regression models are utilized. This methodological approach allows empirical studies to go beyond associations and into the issue of causality (Hoxby 2000). Finally, the approach in Harris et al. (2001) has been followed to study the effects of political institutions and interschool district competition on equity in school district spending. Similar to their approach, school districts have been categorized into quintiles of within-state rankings of school districts' median household income to study the differential effects of political institutions and interschool district competition on spending for districts in each quintile. Previous studies have not taken this particular approach. This approach is innovative because it facilitates investigation of the role of income inequality among school districts in school district spending and student achievement. Overall, this study provides a methodologically rigorous test of theories that will help advance the empirical and theoretical literature on equity in school district spending. Multiple datasets are used including the Popularly Elected Officials Survey data from the US Census Bureau, the Local Education Agency (School District) Longitudinal Finance Survey data, and the School District Demographics System data from the National Center for Education Statistics to examine this dissertation's research questions.

Chapter 1

Funding Inequity in Public Education

A Chronicle of the Debates

Scholarship on public education policy in the United States often expresses different broader policy concerns in the context of centralization and decentralization of school finance and policy. Questions concerning both equity and efficiency of public education system in the United States occupy central space in this scholarship including policy research on school choice, standards, and accountability-based reforms in recent decades. In contextualizing these problems and proposing policy-relevant solutions, researchers have taken different positions on efficiency and normative issues in public education finance in regard to equity and liberty. These debates have produced volumes of articles, books, and evaluation studies in the education policy area.

Subscribing to different views on policy problems and solutions is the usual practice in policy research according to Stone (2002) and Kraft and Furlong (2017). Political ideology is an important factor in divergent views on problem definition (Stone 2002). However, it is important for policy researchers to consider different evaluative and normative criteria in assessing policy alternatives (Kraft and Furlong 2017). When faced with three fundamental assumptions of equality of all educational policy goals, diminishing marginality of spending additional dollar, and inconsistency between different goals, "policymakers must constantly make difficult tradeoffs as they allocate scarce resources" (Godwin and Kemerer 2002, p. 2). In this chapter, I critically discuss various normative and efficiency arguments in the formulation of policy problems and solutions in the context of centralization and decentralization of school finance and policy. Just to reiterate for the readers, centralization of school finance entails existence of fewer school districts through consolidation, whereas the decentralization warrants existence of numerous school districts in the urban regional market for education.

First, I present an overview and evolution of school finance in the United States including institutional and organizational structure of public education. Next, I bring together the theoretical and empirical literature on normative and efficiency issue in the centralization v. decentralization debates in school finance. Policy debates on this topic traverse many contexts. One thread of argument is with regard to the relative merits and drawbacks of decentralized system of public education involving more parental choice and school autonomy over the current centralized system of public education controlled and supervised by school boards and superintendents. I integrate the literature on empirical statements that encompasses allocative efficiency in this context. Another debate in the context of centralization and decentralization in school finance, driven largely by equity and adequacy concerns, is whether state governments should enlarge their roles in school financing. The involvement of judiciary in public school finance is most relevant in this regard. The federal role in addressing concerns in respect of standards and accountability, child poverty, and special needs students is also one of the topics on the centralization debate. Consequently, I integrate the literature on these empirical statements encompassing allocative and productive efficiency. With regard to productive efficiency, researchers have debated whether money matters and how money matters in student learning. The questions in regard to how money matters are essentially the same as evaluation of the efficiency of allocation of school finance on various school resources. This discussion includes an attention to processes through which school inputs are utilized in producing educational outcomes.

AN OVERVIEW OF PUBLIC SCHOOL
SYSTEM IN THE UNITED STATES

In the last fifty years, spending on public schools has tripled in real terms (Peterson 2010, p. 131) and has grown five folds in real dollars over the last century (Godwin and Kemerer 2002). However, this spending has remained flat in the post-recession recovery phase that the US economy is going through and it barely budged by 2.5 percent during the last two decades (Baker 2018). Part of this rise in spending in the last several decades of the last century is explained by rise in teacher salaries, which in real terms rose by about 25 percent between 1960 and 2007 (Peterson 2010). However, among OECD countries, teacher salaries in the United States are still relatively noncompetitive compared to non-teacher salaries (Baker and Weber 2016). Another important reason is the reduction in the number of professional employee per pupil from seventeen in 1960 to eight in 2005 (Peterson 2010). However, the pupil–teacher ratio in 2005 was 15:1. This means that teachers constituted just half the administrative and instructional employees in 2005 (Peterson 2010). The ratio of pupil to support staff also fell by more than half from 59:1 in 1960 to 27:1 in 2006 (Peterson 2010). These trends have remained relatively flat during the last twelve to fourteen years (Baker 2018). These numbers combined with the fact that personnel costs constitute approximately 80 percent of school district budget explain most of the rise in per-pupil spending in real dollars (Peterson 2010) before the onset of a period in which it has remained flat in the last two decades (Baker 2018). Hanushek and Lindseth (2009) also emphasize similar trends in public education spending. Public education has increasingly become a labor-intensive sector over time. At the same time, the rest of the economy is becoming more capital intensive. In such a scenario, the labor-intensive sectors do not make productivity gains, and therefore become more expensive (Baumol 1967; Peterson 2010). But as Baker (2018) notes, teacher wages have remained constant at about 77 percent of non-teacher wages, and thus the argument suggesting the absence of productivity gains on account of rising teacher wages doesn't hold much water. In the international context, the total public expenditure on education in the United States was 6.7 percent of GDP in 2002, which was one of the highest among developed countries (Springer et al. 2008). Taking into account various services for different programs in public education, this level of spending in the United States is comparable to other nations with similar GDP per capita (Baker 2018). Domestically, the public expenditure on K-12 education was roughly 4.7 percent of GDP in 2010 (Springer et al. 2015). The commensurate figure was about 3 percent of GDP in 1960.

On educational outcomes front, the National Assessment of Educational Progress (NAEP) data show that more than one-quarter of students in fourth grade (2007), eighth grade (2007), and twelfth grade (2005) had below basic proficiency in reading tests (Hanushek and Lindseth 2009). In respect of math tests, 18 percent of fourth graders, 29 percent of eighth graders, and 39 percent of twelfth graders registered performance below basic level. In science tests, these percentages were 52, 41, and 46, respectively, for the three grades. The average scores for fourth and eighth grades across all groups in both reading and math are showing consistent upward trend in recent times with the exception of going downward in year 2015 (Baker 2018). The trend in black–white achievement gaps among seventeen-year-olds narrowed until the late 1980s and have remained stagnant since then (Baker 2018; Hanushek and Lindseth 2009). However, during the period 1999–2008, there have been significant achievement gains made by black fourth- and fifth-grade students in math in comparison to white students (Baker 2018). In terms of internationally comparable Programme for International Student Assessment (PISA) tests administered in 2003, only five countries scored below the United States in the list of total thirty countries (Hanushek and Lindseth 2009).

Baker (2018) points that this misdirected comparison is deficient on several accounts, including measurement of financial inputs in education systems in different countries, index for the regional/international differences in the value of education dollar in hiring qualified personnel, and exogenous factors such as economies of scale and population density.

The public education in the United States has also undergone substantial changes in terms of sharing of fiscal burden between local, state, and federal governments over decades. In the early 1930s, more than 80 percent of public school finance came from local sources (Berkman and Plutzer 2005; Mcguire and Papke 2015; Hanushek and Lindseth 2009; Springer et al. 2008). Since the early 1980s, states have stepped up their funding and have exceeded local funding (Hanushek and Lindseth 2009). Currently, about 47 percent of funding comes from state governments, 41 percent comes from the local government, and about 12.7 percent comes from the federal government (Baker 2018; Berkman and Plutzer 2005; Hanushek and Lindseth 2009; Springer et al. 2015). The federal share has increased from about 2 percent in 1940 to 8.5 percent in 2002 to 12.7 percent in 2009 (Gordon 2008, 2015). The passage of the Elementary and Secondary Education Act of 1965 (Title I) has increased federal funding significantly (Hanushek and Lindseth 2009).

The institutional and organizational set up of local school districts has also changed during the nineteenth and twentieth centuries. The number of school districts has declined from over 130,000 in 1930 to about 16,000 in 1970 (Berry 2005). Currently, there are about 15,000 school districts (Baker 2018; Berkman and Plutzer 2005; Howell 2005). Number of public schools has also declined during the twentieth century. From a total of 217,000 in 1920, the number of schools in the United States currently is over 90,000 (Baker 2018; Berry 2005). The average sizes of school districts and schools have also changed. Between 1930 and 2000, the average daily attendance in school increased from 87 to about 480 students. For school districts, the average daily attendance in school increased from 170 to about 2,900 students between 1930 and 2000 (Berry 2005). The size of the school boards also declined as a result of the movement toward a centralized system of schooling in the nineteenth and twentieth centuries (Howell 2005).

The consolidation of school districts is a consequence of larger historical developments in the economic and political structure (Howell 2005). The progressive era embarked on removing politics and inefficiencies on account of corruption and patronage from local and state governments. Howell notes that "Businessmen, professors, and politicians lobbied for the transformation of an agrarian, decentralized pattern of schooling into a bona fide public school system that promoted the values of centralization, efficiency, modernization, and hierarchical control" (Howell 2005, p. 3). The concerns with objectivity and efficiency gave rise to rational control and professionalism (Howell 2005;

Chubb and Moe 1990). The civil service was invented to reward merit and modernity in government sector. These changes mirror the ongoing changes in private economic sectors. Increasing involvement of the state governments in public education finance and policy influenced school district consolidation (Strang 1987). This view on consolidation, however, is a supply-side argument, that is, the progressive leaders supplied those reforms (Fischel 2009). In terms of demand-side perspective, the local residents gave up control over one-room schools in most cases and opted for consolidated, age-graded schools "because the one-room school did not prepare their children for a high school education. Farmers and other rural property owners were penalized if their schools were not 'making the grade' and educating resident children in a more systematic way" (Fischel 2009, p. 2). The penalty was in the form of lowered property values.

In recent times, there is some movement back toward decentralized system of schooling based on school autonomy and parental choice. The examples include charter schools, magnet schools, and vouchers. For instance, the first charter school program was introduced in Minnesota in 1991, and since then forty-two states and the District of Columbia have instituted charter school legislation (Bifulco and Bulkley 2015; Peterson 2010). Currently, there are about 5,000 charter schools in the United States (Baker 2018). Publicly funded school voucher programs have also been instituted in Milwaukee, Cleveland, and Florida (Zimmer and Bettinger 2015). The following section discusses pertinent normative and efficiency issues in the debate over centralization and decentralization in public education.

NORMATIVE AND EFFICIENCY ISSUES IN THE CENTRALIZATION V. DECENTRALIZATION DEBATE

In the context of the federal system of governments in the United States, the authority and responsibility for public education rest with the state governments (Gordon 2015; Springer et al. 2015). Most state constitutions explicitly guarantee free school education (Berkman and Plutzer 2005) and many state constitutions require equitable provision for all its children (Mickelson 2003). States, with the exception of Hawaii, have delegated major responsibility for operating and financing public schools to local school districts (Gordon 2015; Springer et al. 2015; Belfield and Levin 2005b). Hawaii has a statewide public education system. From a comparative international perspective, the United States has a decentralized public education system (Gordon 2015).

This decentralized public education system, as looked upon from the international perspective, was significantly more decentralized at the turn of the twentieth century (Berkman and Plutzer 2005; Howell 2005; Peterson 2010; Chubb and Moe 1990). The earlier education system until the early nineteenth century was largely private, local, and religious (Odden and Picus 2013). The opponents of present system of public education have viewed the earlier system as a decentralized education system (Chubb and Moe 1990, p. 3; Peterson 2010). In recent decades, however, school education finance and governance have become more centralized (Howell 2005; Gordon 2015). The power has shifted from local districts to states, because states are shouldering more fiscal burdens than the local governments. The federal role has also expanded (Gordon 2015). This increased centralization is largely a consequence of dependence of local governments on state and federal governments for money and the institution of performance and accountability standards in the last two decades (Gordon 2015; Corcoran and Evans 2015). The equity and adequacy lawsuits have also aided this centralization. The proponents of school choice hope that the recent technological advancements would push the current centralized system of public education to a truly decentralized system in future. The labor-intensive nature of public education would also undergo transformation in such a systemic change (Peterson 2010, p. 19).

At the same time as the public education in the United States was going through rapid institutional and organizational restructuring, the policy-relevant normative and efficiency arguments assumed different forms and meaning in different contexts, although consistent with the initial broader policy goals (Guthrie and Wong 2015; Odden and Picus 2013). The current public education system started taking shape from the 1850s. The movement toward the current system of public common schools was to ensure constitutionally guaranteed liberties. The Progressive-era reformers thought of education as a means to prepare citizenry to participate as equals in affairs of the government (Odden and Picus 2013; Springer et al. 2015). The creation of free common schools shifted control over education from individuals and church to the state. "Control over schools was a problematic aspect in crafting statewide, education systems. The resolution to the control issue was creation of local, lay boards of education that, it was argued, would function in the place of parents and church" (Odden and Picus 2000, p. 9). This type of local control took away the control of education from family and community and gave it to more centralized institutions under the control of professionals (Peterson 2010; Moe 2001). The efficiency would have also accrued from increasing average size of schools and school districts (Moe 2001, p. 32). The one "consistent model of governance and administration" would also be efficient and capable in managing external funds and intergovernmental programs (Moe 2001). This move toward "one best system" was to expunge inefficiency, promote standardization apart from ensuring the egalitarian and normative principles of liberty and equity (Chubb and Moe 1990; Peterson 2010). While the egalitarian and normative principles of liberty and equity form one of the core goals of any policy, efficiency in itself is not a policy goal (Stone 2002). However, efficiency is an important and key criterion to judge alternative policies. This is because public policy involves distribution of scarce resources. The normative and egalitarian conceptions of liberty and equity are, however, very difficult to reconcile because these concepts mean different things to different people and because pursuit of one restricts attainment of the other (Guthrie and Wong 2015). Furthermore, each of the three principles of liberty, equity, and efficiency is constantly in competition with the other two (Guthrie and Wong 2015). For example, "Liberty, which is the ability of individuals and groups to choose and to maximize personal preferences, is often seen as the higher goal. Unfettered choice in schooling, however, might jeopardize civic unity or social cohesion and could exacerbate material and social inequality" (Guthrie and Wong 2015, p. 63). The examples concerning the pursuit of educational equality in the United States include legislations, such as the Elementary and Secondary Education Act of 1965 and the No Child Left Behind Act of 2001, and state court school finance equalization decisions, such as *Serrano v. Priest in California* and *Robinson v. Cahill,* in New Jersey (Guthrie and Wong 2015). Pursuit of liberty and efficiency has not been relegated to inferior place in policy consideration. "For example, tax limitation movements, charter school and voucher proposals, and demand for greater market play in education have been on the policy agenda at all levels of government since the 1980s. Contemporary concern for efficiency and productivity in the education system is also evident in components of the NCLB, federal Teacher Incentive Fund legislation, and state pay-for-performance teacher pay plans" (Guthrie and Wong 2015, p. 63).

However, equity, efficiency, choice, and exercise of preferences are intricately related with various shades of political philosophy of liberty. In the context of a "liberal democratic society," such as the United States, Godwin and Kemerer (2002) identify three important policy goals for education that are essential for ensuring liberty. (1) In order to become economically independent, students should learn economic skills. (2) The students should also learn the political skills and understandings in order to participate in the democratic process in a meaningful way. (3) The students should not only learn moral reasoning for understanding differences between ethical and unethical behaviors, they should also be able to appreciate the importance of such behaviors for a good society. The contemporary liberalism includes the policy goal of equal educational opportunity along with above three dimensions of liberty (Godwin and Kemerer 2002). Essentially, the Equality of Educational Opportunity is a necessary vehicle to attain the above three policy goals. This is evident in the authors' own words:

> Contemporary liberalism maintains that public funding of education is the chief mechanism the state uses to reduce the inequalities in economic and social rewards created by the circumstances of birth and childhood. If the rational application of skills is a necessary condition for achieving rewards, then a just education policy will provide students with equal opportunities to develop rationality and to obtain skills. (Godwin and Kemerer 2002, p. 2)

Equal educational opportunity is not a one-dimensional concept. One view on equal educational opportunity is that "everyone is treated the same way within the school house and each is given instruction appropriate to his or her ability, so that all are given the same chance to build on the capabilities they bring to the school floor" (Woessmann and Peterson 2007, p. 4). An alternate, more liberal and expansive view is that schools should "remedy the deficiencies that some children bring with them to school so that only random chance determines which members of the next generation rise to the highest positions of society." These different conceptions of equal educational opportunities have different interpretations in regard to both the input and outcome side of public education finance. However, Equality of Educational Opportunity is a balance between the classical liberal freedom and full equal liberty (Ericson 1984). This is consistent with views about contemporary liberalism (Ericson 1984; Godwin and Kemerer 2002). The pursuit of full-blown equality of liberty requires institution of the totalitarian state instead of the liberal state. This scenario is counter to the notion of individual liberty. Only a totalitarian bureaucracy can undertake massive redistribution to ensure full equal liberty (Ericson 1984).

There are different shades of liberalism that see the goals of public education and the distribution of power between parents and the state differently (Godwin and Kemerer 2002, p. 91). These conceptions of liberalism can be viewed in terms of relative strengths of the roles of the state and parents. These liberal ideals also highlight the struggle for balance between various degrees of individual freedom, choice and well-being, and local control, on the one hand, and the role of the state and individuals in the pursuit of political, social, and economic equity through public education, on the other. Post-classical liberalism has permitted greater state control in education. Concomitantly, the right of parents over control of the content of education has substantially diminished (Godwin and Kemerer 2002).

Classical liberals proposed minimal role of the state in education, but they agreed that the state should administer tests for literacy and numeracy. Mill suggested that state should fund education of those not able to afford school fees, but the state should desist from providing it directly. Parents should have control over the content of the education including lessons on morality. The overall goal of education should be to impart "Practical skills for economic self-sufficiency and self-government." Mill also thought that education should promote the development of tolerance and autonomy. Political liberals prescribed that the goal of education should encompass the "development of tolerant citizens and the necessary skills for self-government, economic self-sufficiency, and the performance of citizen duties." Political liberals view educational opportunity as a key to achieve social and political equality. Toward this goal, the state should fund and regulate education. However, the state should not provide education as a monopoly. The state should also not regulate private schools. The parents, on the other hand, could "Control that portion of education dealing with what constitutes a good life and a good person." Parents have a diminished role in comparison to their role under classical liberal state.

In comprehensive liberals' view, apart from funding and providing public schools, the state should also strictly regulate private schools to achieve economic and political equality. This view requires the state to ensure greater degree of economic and political equality in comparison to classical and political liberalism. Comprehensive liberals are for stricter state control over individual liberty. They would like the state to eliminate all forms of discrimination. Parents violating constitutional rules in this regard should not go unpunished. In this view, a life based on faith is inferior, and comprehensive liberals would like to use publicly funded schools to socialize students to this idea. The progressive liberals, on the other hand, would like the state to pursue much broader educational goals and to exercise total control over schooling. The common schools should be the means to socialize students to a common culture so that they become democratic citizens and form a liberal democratic society. Dewey and his followers viewed parental role as supporters of decisions taken by the state and professional educators. The state should also proactively eliminate other social inequities and illiberal conditions. The common public school system is a key resource at state's disposal in realizing these social goals.

Finally, communitarians view that an individual citizen is incapable of understanding the "conception of the good person and the good life" (Godwin and Kemerer 2002, p. 92). Therefore, while guaranteeing various liberal individual rights the state should use collective institutions "to deliberate and develop social conceptions of these ideals" (Godwin and Kemerer 2002, p. 92). The state should use education to socialize people in pursuit of wider acceptance and realization of those socially created goals. The parental role in this type of society and public education is merely as supporters of decisions taken by the state through deliberative democracy.

In the context of contemporary public school finance in the United States, Monk has argued that equity and local control can coexist. This coexistence pertains to the process of distribution of educational resources by the state across school districts for achieving equity without undermining the promotion of local control and autonomy of the schools (Ericson 1984, p. 99). Monk employs the concept of fiscal neutrality in this regard. Fiscal neutrality means that "the quality of a child's education shall not be a function of wealth, other than the wealth of the state as a whole." In Ericson's words: "Fiscal neutrality is achieved when state mandates produce equity in school district opportunities. . . . Local control is achieved when school district spending variations are the product of only pure, legitimate tastes, if any such exist. Thus, equity and local control can coexist" (Ericson 1984, p. 100). In reference to the classical liberal state, Bull is of the view that local control and autonomy over public education is justified only if this type of arrangement can "secure either personal or participatory liberty." Under these criteria, Bull concludes that "local control of the schools cannot be justified in terms of securing either liberty-related value." Therefore, decision making for public education in the United States should rest with more centralized state. Consequently, a federally controlled system of schools is the best.

These debates over promotion of political, social, and economic ideals of a liberal democratic society through equity in public education with varying degrees of state and parental control are even more apparent in the literature on school choice. The issue of school choice is important in school finance because it not only involves public funding of private schools but also because school choice and the resultant competition affects productive use of school resources (Gill and Booker 2015). There are key arguments on both sides of the school choice debate (Belfield and Levin 2005a, 2005b; Levin 2015; Peterson 2010; Betts and Loveless 2005; Godwin and Kemerer 2002; Moe 2001). Godwin and Kemerer (2002) have critically summarized the theoretical debates and testable empirical statements on both sides of the argument. The impact of school choice on urban inner-city children is also a key issue in the debate (Godwin and Kemerer 2002).

The school choice has always existed in the United States in two forms (Betts and Loveless 2005; Belfield and Levin 2005b; Peterson 2010). Parents have always had the right to choose private school for their child or teach them at home. The residential choice of parents also reflects a choice of schools for their child. The latter is in-egalitarian because it has resulted in residential segregation in terms of socioeconomic status (SES) and race (Peterson 2010). On the other hand, proponents argue that this type of "Tiebout sorting" is both equitable and efficient (Hoxby 1996; Godwin and Kremerer 2002). In recent decades, school choice includes magnet schools, charter schools, and vouchers (Betts and Loveless 2005; Peterson 2010).

The debate on school choice began in earnest with the work of Milton Friedman on government's role in public education production and provision (Friedman 1955, 1962). Friedman opined that the government should fund public education through vouchers that should be given directly to the parents and that the provision of education should be left to the private schools. However, consistent with the social goals of education, the government should formulate and set minimum standards for the private schools and enforce them. This policy suggestion was to realize efficiency gains on account of competition in private market of education, and at the same time, fulfilling the social goals of education. Competition between schools in attracting and retaining students would result in cost reductions, less bureaucracy, and efficiency. Under this policy option, the control of education was to move from the state to parents and private schools. The market mechanism is supposed to ensure consumer sovereignty. This idea is consistent with the advancement of individual liberty because parents could choose from among schools for their child that matched their values. In recent decades, Chubb and Moe (1990) have reinvigorated the interest on school choice. Since then, this has been a well-researched area. The proponents and opponents of school choice have taken positions along the following key issues (Godwin and Kemerer 2002; Betts and Loveless 2005).

First, the proponents of school choice and competition argue that schools would operate more efficiently if their survival hinges on increased competition among schools for students. Second, with a menu of different types of schools to choose from, the less affluent parents and their child will no longer be at a disadvantage The loosening of democratic control is also beneficial to less affluent and minority students that disproportionately reside in inner-city of urban areas (Chubb and Moe 1990; Godwin and Kemerer 2002). There should be special safeguards in the design of school choice programs with regard to the inner-city schools and choice programs in general (Godwin and Kemerer 2002; Betts and Loveless 2005; Levin 2015). The design issue is also very important from the public policy perspective in school finance (Levin 2008; Belfield and Levin 2005b; Moe 2005). Third, democratic control is wasteful and a barrier in school productivity. Bureaucratic structure and democratic control in public schools are inherently inefficient and slow down student performance (Chubb and Moe 1988, 1990). Fourth, the democratic control breeds unclear missions and goals, and reduces coordination and teamwork among administrators, faculty, and staff. There is reduction in teacher autonomy and satisfaction under the democratically controlled public schools. Finally, the market of schools would cater to the diverse needs of students in a better manner than the current centralized system of public schools.

The opponents of school choice have raised questions on freedom of choice, productive efficiency, equity, social cohesion, and organizational grounds (Levin 2015; Meier 2000). Less educated and lower SES parents face difficulty in exercising choice due to lack of timely information, networks, and transportation (Levin 2015). On the productive efficiency ground, opponents argue that competition will benefit just the "best" students. Students with greater needs will find themselves in segregated school environments with more like them in terms of ethnicity and SES (Orfield and Yun 1999; Levin 2015; Wells 1993; Fiske and Ladd 2000; Epple and Romano 2000; Schneider et al. 1997). On social cohesion grounds, opponents argue that private schools would undermine the common purpose of schooling in their pursuit of making narrow gains in the market (Wolfe 2003; Gill and Booker 2015; Levin 2015). Meier et al. (2000) argue that bureaucracy increases as schools take actions that are linked to improved performance, in a response to Chubb and Moe. This implies that bureaucracy is a consequence of lower academic performance and not a causal factor.

The empirical evidence on the effect of school competition on student achievement and other public purposes of education, such as student integration, is mixed (Belfield and Levin 2005b; Gill and Booker 2015). All these results, however, address different policy issues most directly because school choice entails reorganization in allocation of the public school finance. In light of conflicting evidence and unintended consequences, the debate over school choice reforms between political liberals and progressive liberals is poised to continue in future. The extant theoretical and empirical literatures do not establish that school choice policies are superior to the current form of centralized education finance and policies. Moreover, scholars in the progressive liberal tradition have found the current system of school finance wanting on equity and adequacy grounds, although states have been somewhat successful in addressing funding disparity when directed by state courts to do so (Baker 2018). These scholars and their legal colleagues have successfully used the state judicial system to bring in more equitable school finance. The education finance and policy issues raised by these scholars are consistent with Monk's contention about the coexistence of local control and state finance on fiscal neutrality principle and Bull's views about more centralization (Ericson 1984). Baker (2018), Odden and Picus (2013), Springer et al. (2015), Baker and Green (2015), Downes and Stiefel (2015), Duncombe and Yinger (2015), Hanushek and Lindseth (2009), Hanushek (2006), and West and Peterson (2007) comprehensively present the academic debate over equity and adequacy of school finance and judiciary's involvement.

The partial dependence of school finance on local revenue has been the root cause of disparities in per-pupil spending across school districts. Rich districts can raise more revenue at a lower tax rate, whereas a poor district cannot raise enough revenue even with higher property tax rate. This is because rich districts have higher property wealth per pupil or tax base. This double disadvantage is against the egalitarian principles of equality of educational opportunities and equal protection to child (Baker 2018; Springer et al. 2015; Berkman and Plitzer 2005; Odden and Picus 2013). This inequity exists among districts both within and between states (Baker 2018; Godwin and Kemerer 2002; Murray et al. 1998; Berkman and Plutzer 2005). Moreover, the funding disparities between the states are relatively larger than within them (Murray, Evans and Schwab 1998; Corcoran and Evans 2015; Berkman and Plutzer 2005; Moe 2001).

In attempting to address this inequity, states have used different funding formulas over the twentieth century. But the disparities in school district spending have persisted because these funding mechanisms had drawbacks, and states continued to allow local resources for public education (Springer et al. 2015; Odden and Picus 2013; Koski and Hahnel 2015; Hoxby 1998; Wong 1999; Hertert, Busch, and Odden 1994). However, apart from the local wealth, other local factors also explain funding disparities across school districts. The factors comprise local political, economic, regional, and demographic characteristics.

Public taste for education spending, old age population, teachers' union, and school board composition influence budgetary allocation of the local school district (Berkman and Plutzer 2005). Also, individuals choose to live in the community with a mixture of tax–expenditure bundle that matches their preferences and budgets (Tiebout 1956; Harris et al. 2001; Poterba 1997). Arguably, this is the efficient choice of levels of goods and services made by the residents within a local jurisdiction while making residential choices (Godwin and Kemerer 2002; Gill and Booker 2015; Peterson 2010). This choice level matches median-voter's preferences (Fischel 2001; Godwin and Kemerer 2002). The levels of taxation and spending of local governments are a function of relationship of levels of interjurisdictional competition (Brennan and Buchanan 1980; Oates 1985; Nelson 1986; Poterba 1994, 1996; Merrifield 1991, 2000; Craw 2008). However, appropriate type of local government plays key role in minimizing inflated public budgets and inefficiencies in local taxation and spending (Craw 2008; Frant 1996; Feiock, Jeong, and Kim 2003; Jimenez and Hendrick 2010).

The existence of school funding disparities, however, is against the principle of providing equal educational opportunities to children. Employing the equity principles of fiscal neutrality and equal protection, the proponents of equity in public education have pleaded the judiciary to direct federal and state governments to address fiscal disparities and ensure equality of educational opportunities (Koski and Hahnel 2015). Proponents have used education clauses in state constitution and legislations (Mickelson 2003; West and Peterson 2007). The next chapter discusses these court-mandated education finance reforms in greater detail.

EQUITY AND EFFICIENCY IN
CONTEMPORARY SCHOOL FINANCE

The issue of differential educational outcomes in terms of ethnicity, region, and socioeconomic status has been one of the main discourses on public education finance. Various policy solutions suggested for addressing the problem of inequitable funding in school districts get fillip if it can be shown that money matters in bridging gaps in educational outcomes. The debate over the relationship between money and educational outcomes also includes how best money could be distributed across various school inputs. There is a large body of literature exploring the relationship between school finance or resources that money can buy and students' academic achievement. I recommend readers to read Baker (2018) for a comprehensive review of the latest literature. I summarize the key threads in the debate over this topic in the following.

The studies fall in one of the two broader policy positions. One position says that money does not matter in educational outcomes because of inefficiencies in resource use, that is, various school inputs on which money is allocated are not producing gains in educational achievement. This argument does not mean that money does not matter at all. It only means that additional resources are being wasteful (Hanushek 1989a, 1989b, 1991, 1994, 1996a, 1996b). The other position is that money does matter for gains in educational outcomes and that high level of funding is crucial in providing smaller classrooms, schools, and more qualified teachers various other school resources (Greenwald et al. 1996; Hedges and Greenwald 1996; Hedges et al. 1994). Questioning Hanushek's methodology as mere "vote-counting," Krueger (2002) finds that other approaches to weighting effect sizes lead to more consistent and positive effect of school resources on student achievement. Burtless (1996) and Elliot (1998) have critically summarized the two opposing arguments. Elliot finds that "per-pupil expenditures indirectly increase students' achievement by giving students access to educated teachers who use effective pedagogies in the classroom" (Elliot 1998, p. 223). Per-pupil expenditures for instruction and the administration of school districts significantly affect students' achievement (Wenglinsky 1997).

The above debate over the importance of school finance in educational achievement has its origin in Equality of Educational Opportunity study done in 1966 by Coleman et al. (1966). Coleman and his colleagues reported the controversial finding that school resources were least effective in influencing student learning in comparison to home resources and peers. However, a study by Borman and Dowling (2010), using the same Equality of Educational Opportunity study data with more advanced and contemporary multilevel regression technique, finds that two-fifth of the variation in student achievement is explained by variation in resources across schools.

Class size is an important school resource that money can influence. But there is no agreement among researchers that smaller class size is better for student learning (Rice and Schwartz 2015). However, smaller class size may benefit specific group of students, subject matters, and teachers in special circumstances (Hanushek 2002; Aaronson et al. 2007). The Tennessee STAR class size experiment also could not resolve the general disagreement. Finn and Achilles (1999) and Nye et al. (1999) reported positive effect of reduction in class size. Hanushek (1999), however, argued that the experiment was contaminated. Specifically, the contamination produced unmeasured differences between the students in small and large classes leading to unreliable results. Another important school resource is teacher quality. Research shows that quality of teachers is positively related to student achievement (Rivkin et al. 1998; Sanders 1998). There is, however, lack of agreement on specific teacher qualifications that raise student achievement the most (Hansuhek 2010; Nye et al. 2004; Wayne and Youngs 2003).

While studying the education finance and outcome relationships, it is also important to explore the role of educational processes (Rice and Schwartz 2015; Grubb 2009). Researchers look into the internal workings of schools and school systems to explain disparities in educational outcomes. For example, Condron and Roscigno note that "specific attributes of schools may be important mediators between spending and achievement" (Condron and Roscigno 2003, p. 19). This explains the contradictory findings on the relationship between education funding and education outcome. Similarly, Borman and Dowling (2010) find that student achievement gaps between African American and white students and between higher and lower SES students within schools are partly attributable to teachers' biases that favor middle-class students and to schools' greater reliance on curriculum differentiation through the use of academic and nonacademic tracking after controlling for students' family background. These findings point to the fact that larger processes and structures prevalent in the society exert influence over school processes and hence educational outcome. Mickelson (2003), Roscigno et al. (2006), Condron and Roscigno (2003), Ladd et al. (1999), Grubb (2009), Condron (2009), and Roza (2010) underscore the importance of looking deeper into the inner workings of schools, school systems, urban environment, and school finance from an equity perspective for explaining inequitable educational outcomes.

As a proponent of adequate public education, Baker (2018) has forcefully argued with the aid of comprehensive analysis of more recent data that not only money matters, equitable distribution of money by taking into account of group, and place-specific disadvantages also matters. He comes hard on those who oppose more funding for public education. Baker (2018, p. 53) notes that:

the following five sources of evidence no longer have a legitimate place in the debate over state school finance policy and whether and how money matters in K-12 education:

- vote counts of correlational studies between spending and outcomes without regard for rigor of the analyses and quality of the data on which they depend;
- the long-term trend argument that shows long-term spending going up and NAEP scores staying flat;
- international comparisons asserting that the United States spends more than other developed countries but achieves less on international assessments;
- anecdotal assertions that states like New Jersey and cities like Kansas City provide proof that massive infusions of funding have proven ineffective at improving student outcomes; and
- the assertion that how money is spent is much more important than how much is available.

Baker (2018, p. 101) goes on to argue that the following key findings explain the current state of school finance systems in the United States.

Rigorous, well-designed, and policy-relevant empirical research finds that:

- Money matters for schools and in determining school quality and student outcomes. More specifically, substantive, sustained, and targeted school finance reforms can significantly boost short-term and long-run student outcomes and reduce gaps among low-income students and their more advantaged peers.
- Money matters in commonsense ways. Increased funding provides for additional staff, including reduced class sizes, longer school days and years, and more competitive compensation.
- Cuts do cause harm. The equity of student outcomes is eroded by reducing equity of real resources across children of varied economic backgrounds.

CONCLUDING REMARKS

The educational policy in the United States has attempted to tackle normative and efficiency issues through both centralization and decentralization approaches. Policymakers have consistently tried to address some version of equality and efficiency in public education from time to time. The public education in the United States has undergone substantial transformation over the past one-and-a-half centuries. The current system of public education through a mix of federal, state, and local control is more centralized than the proponents of school choice theory would like to have. This concern has arisen mainly in response to the supposed failure of the public schools in addressing inequities in educational outcomes in spite of rising expenditures. However, such blanket assertions do not hold in recent studies when these studies take into account contextual factors in their analysis of data (Baker 2018). School reform policies consistent with school choice are suggested as alternative ways to look at school finance for improving efficiency.

School choice in terms of home schooling, private schools, and residential choice has always existed. Some scholars favor residential choice, while others find it inequitable in school finance. School choice reform creates market-type schools so that parents have arguably more choice and schools have autonomy. Proponents argue that through program design, school choice programs can protect inner-city students from disadvantages on account of ethnicity and SES. In recent decades, more market-like schools in the form of charter schools, vouchers, and magnet schools have come up. However, there is no conclusive evidence on positive impact of such reform policies on educational outcomes. In fact, empirical evidence suggests that these policies have led to resegregation. Also, the theoretical and empirical literatures have not conclusively established the supremacy of school choice policies over the current form of education finance. The debate over centralization and decentralization of school finance is poised to continue.

Moreover, progressive liberals have vigorously questioned the current system of school finance on equity and adequacy grounds. They argue that disparity in education spending across school districts is a great impediment in affording a child equal opportunity to succeed in life. These scholars and their legal colleagues have successfully used the state judicial system to bring in more equitable school finance. This strategy was in response to the failure of various attempts by the state governments in addressing inequity in school finance through different funding formulas. The federal role in terms of standards and accountability-based reforms also aided the adequacy movement.

With regard to productive efficiency, the researchers have debated whether money matters and how money matters in student learning. The questions in regard to how money matters are essentially the same as evaluation of the efficiency of allocation of school finance on various school resources. This discussion includes an attention to processes through which school inputs are utilized in producing educational outcomes. The empirical evidence is mixed. Studies using more contemporary methodologies and broader meaning of education finance, however, find evidence that money matters and that the processes through which school resources are allocated to students also matters. From public policy perspective, an investigation of broader processes in school finance is also important in formulating appropriate policies for better educational outcomes through reorganization of school finance.

Chapter 2

Government's Role in Addressing Funding Disparities

Since the beginning of the progressive era in the 1850s, the role of the state in public education has gradually expanded with the objective of providing standardized, efficient, equitable, and common education to each child (Chubb and Moe 1990; Howell 2005; Levin 2015; Springer et al. 2015). The US public education, however, has not been able to overcome twin challenges of inequitable provisioning in education and inequitable educational outcomes. There is a lot of variation in per-pupil funding across school districts in the United States (Berkman and Plutzer 2005). As noted earlier, the rich suburban districts spend more money than poor urban school districts because the former enjoy higher per-pupil property wealth. Rich districts can raise more revenue at a lower tax rate, whereas a poor district cannot raise enough revenue even with higher property-tax rate. This double disadvantage is a major roadblock in according equitable and adequate educational opportunities and equal protection to the child (Springer et al. 2015; Berkman and Plutzer 2005; Odden and Picus 2013). The poor urban school districts have disproportionately high proportions of minority and other disadvantaged students who require additional resources for specialized programs and staff (Moe 2001). At the same time, the educational outcomes are also unequal in general and along ethnic and SES lines in particular (Baker 2018; Hanushek and Lindseth 2009), though there is evidence of significant gains in academic achievement among minority students in comparison to white students (Baker 2018). Scholars and policymakers have debated these issues on the input side, the outcome side, and their interrelationships in a very comprehensive manner. This debate has generated a lot of research and many policy prescriptions.

First, I provide an overview of funding inequity in public education and state governments' attempt to reduce inequitable education finance. These attempts were based on different conceptions of equity in finance and funding

formulas. Subsequently, I discuss the evolution of equity and adequacy lawsuits in response to disparities in school district finance. I spell out the equity
concerns and bring together developments until most recently. I include the
discussion on importance of performance standards and the federal initiatives
in this regard. The role of costing studies in suggesting adequate finance is
also discussed. I briefly discuss the impact of equity and adequacy lawsuits
on equity in school district finance. Next, I discuss the literature that has cri-
tiqued equity and adequacy lawsuits-based reform. I also critically analyze the
alternative school finance reforms that have been suggested. Subsequently, I
contextualize the student, family, school, and societal-level forces that foster
unequal educational outcomes within the context of regional socioeconomic
processes. This chapter then concludes.

INEQUITY IN FUNDING AND
ADDRESSING FUNDING DISPARITY

The US Constitution has not explicitly provided any federal jurisdiction
over education, and at the same time, the Tenth Amendment has reserved
all residual rights for the states. Therefore, the authority and responsibility
for public education rest with the state governments (Gordon 2015; Springer
et al. 2015). Most state constitutions explicitly pledge free school education
(Berkman and Plutzer 2005) and many state constitutions require equitable
provision for all its children (Mickelson 2003). Constitutions and relevant
legislations of all states, with the exception of Hawaii, have delegated major
responsibility for operating and financing public schools to local school districts (Gordon 2015; Springer et al. 2015; Belfield and Levin 2005). Hawaii
has a statewide public education system. From a comparative international
perspective, the United States has a fairly decentralized public education
system (Gordon 2015). Because local governments are the creature of the
states (Peterson 1981), in most cases, states have given political authority to
school districts to raise local resources for providing K-12 education within
their jurisdictions. However, a significant number of school districts have no
fiscal authority and they must rely on the state or other local governments for
funding (Berkman and Plutzer 2005). The local school districts in most cases
raise revenue from local property taxes (Baker 2018; Picus et al. 2015).

The fiscal burden of public education is shared between local, state, and
federal governments. Up until the late 1970s and early 1980s, revenue
from local property tax was the major source of funding for school districts
(Berkman and Plutzer 2005; Mcguire and Papke 2015). At the beginning of
the 1930s, more than 80 percent of public school finance came from local
sources (Hanushek and Lindseth 2009). However, for the last more than three

decades, the states' funding has overtaken the local funding of K-12 education in the United States (Baker 2018; Berkman and Plutzer 2005; Hanushek and Lindseth 2009; Springer et al. 2015). The federal share has also increased from about 2 percent in 1940 to 12.7 percent in 2009 (Gordon 2015). The passage of the Elementary and Secondary Education Act of 1965 (Title I) has increased federal funding significantly (Hanushek and Lindseth 2009).

In the last fifty years, the rising level of expenditure has not resulted in commensurate substantial reduction in funding disparities across school districts (Fiske and Ladd 2015; Godwin and Kemerer 2002; Berkman and Plutzer 2005). After controlling for regional variation in prices, the per-pupil spending varied from $9360 in New Jersey, to $8,860 in New York, to roughly $4,580 in Utah. The per-pupil spending differences between states are largely due to disparities in wealth, population, political culture, and policy choices of states (Hochschild and Scovronick 2003).

Building on the four measures of inequality in per-pupil spending in school districts in the United States developed by Murray et al. (1998), a recent study reports improvements in funding equity between 1972 and 2011 (Corcoran and Evans 2015). Almost two-thirds of the variation in per-pupil spending across school districts is explained by difference in funding between states (Murray et al. 1998; Corcoran and Evans 2015; Godwin and Kemerer 2002). Hanushek and Lindseth (2009) attribute this disparity to the fact that although the various funding formulas employed by states increase spending by poor districts, they do not impact rich district's capacity to spend even higher amounts. In the current system of public education based on local control, a major source of school finance comes mostly from local property tax (Koski and Hahnel 2015; Springer et al. 2015). The tax rate, property values, and student population decide the level of local revenue and hence cause great variation in spending (Berkman and Plutzer 2005; Odden and Picus 2013).

The proponents have argued for reduction in inequity in spending across school districts for addressing unequal educational outcomes. The proponents would like to ensure equality in educational opportunity so that every child has equal chance of succeeding in life (Baker 2018; Peterson 2010). These arguments have their origin in the study on equity in school finance by Elwood P. Cubberley's in the early twentieth century (Odden and Picus 2013; Springer et al. 2015). Cubberley argued that equity in distribution of school finance was relatively more important than just spending more money (Cubberley 1905).

Initially, states allocated equal amounts of money called flat grant to address this inequity. This grant to the school districts on per-school basis did not consider the number of students and local tax base (Springer et al. 2015). Consequently, many states instituted minimum foundation plans (Odden and Picus 2013; Springer et al. 2015). Apart from ensuring a minimum base level spending, this plan gave more money to school districts with lower per-pupil property-tax base in comparison to districts with a large property-tax base per pupil. This plan also failed to equalize differences in local fiscal capacity (Odden and Picus 2013; Springer et al. 2015). Recently, some states have adopted percentage equalizing plan (Odden and Picus 2013; Springer et al. 2015). This plan defines equity as equal access to school finance and ensures that "district level effort to support schools is equally rewarded regardless of any individual district's property wealth" (Springer et al. 2008, p. 10). However, this plan has built-in disincentives for raising local revenue effort, and there is the possibility that some districts, instead of receiving money from the state, may end up making payments to the state. Until 2005, only nine states have adopted guaranteed tax base program. A total of thirty-four states still rely on foundation programs, and five states are using weighted funding based on census percentages. North Carolina had a heavily modified grant program, and Hawaii had a statewide funding system (Springer et al. 2015).

The federal government has also influenced school finance and policy in several ways. In *Brown v. Board of Education*, the US Supreme Court ended the school segregation in 1954. Title VI of Civil Rights Act of 1964 in conjunction with Title I of Elementary and Secondary Education Act (ESEA) of 1965 providing compensatory funds to school districts based on child poverty also helped in desegregation. Sufficient funds under Title I of the ESEA made the Title VI of Civil rights act more effective (Gordon 2015). In recent decades, many states have instituted performance standards for students and schools along with mechanisms for ensuring accountability in the wake of Improving America's Schools Act, 1994. This legislation reflects federal government's support and concern for the standard-based reforms in the aftermath of the publication of *A National at Risk* in 1983. The No Child Left Behind Act of 2001 has further emphasized these standards, and accountability and is more stringent in this regard.

In spite of state governments' efforts at funding equalization, there still exist intrastate differences in funding (Baker 2018; Odden and Picus 2013; Hoxby 1998; Wong 1999; Hertert et al. 1994). The existence of school funding disparities, although explained by place, economics, politics, and demographic factors (Harris et al. 2001; Poterba 1997; Oates 1985; Nelson 1986; Poterba 1994, 1996; Merrifield 1991, 2000; Craw 2008; Brennan and Buchanan 1980; Frant 1996; Feiock et al. 2003), is against the principle of providing equal educational opportunities to children (Chemerinsky 2003). The dissatisfaction with this type of fiscal disparities has propelled some scholars and their legal colleagues to seek increased control and funding of schools from states. For example, Chemerinsky (2003) advocates for the creation of school districts coterminous with the metropolitan area boundary to remove inequity in education funding. The equity principles employed in advocating for more centralized education finance are equality in per-pupil spending or horizontal equity, needs-based funding equality or vertical equity, equal opportunity for an equal outcome or effective equality, and fiscal neutrality (Koski and Hahnel 2015).

EQUITY AND ADEQUACY LAWSUITS
IN EDUCATION FINANCE

Two studies came up around the same time with powerful legal arguments in support of ensuring equality of educational opportunities. In combination with Fourteenth Amendment's equal protection clause, these studies came up with the constitutional argument that property-dependent school spending disparities within states was an injustice (Wise 1968; Coons et al. 1970). Whereas, Wise (1968) held the notion that money spent on a child should not depend on geographic accident and socioeconomic status of parents. Coons et al. (1970) emphasized that money spent on a child should be independent of local community's wealth. Wise (1968) advocated for equal per-pupil spending across school districts, that is, horizontal equity. This principle of "one scholar, one dollar" did not take into account place-specific cost differentials in providing education (Koski and Hahnel 2015). Fiscal neutrality principle (Coons et al. 1970) implies that local district's wealth should not be a decisive factor in the quality of schooling a child receives, over and above the wealth of the state as a whole (Springer et al. 2015; Ericson 1984, Odden and Picus 2013). This equality principle did not emphasize equal per-pupil spending across school districts, thereby making room for variation in the cost of providing education. The two equity principles also did not require showing relationship between education spending and educational outcomes (Koski and Hahnel 2015).

There are two other equity principles applicable to the current system of school finance. One is vertical equity applicable in case of special needs students. Horowitz argued that school finance system is inequitable if it fails to "adequately compensate for the inadequate educational preparation of culturally deprived children" and instead provides same educational programs and services in all schools (Horowitz 1966, p. 1148). This equity principle requires a student-by-student measurement of resource requirement and remedy and hence is difficult to manage (Koski and Hahnel 2015). Under the concept of equal opportunity for an equal outcome or effective equity, the state has an obligation to provide equal educational opportunity to a child (Kirp 1968). This obligation is satisfied only if each child has an equal chance for an equal educational outcome, irrespective of the child's socioeconomic background and differences in cost or effort in providing such an education

(Ladd et al. 1999; Koski and Hahnel 2015). Effective equality is theoretically close to adequacy lawsuits (Koski and Hahnel 2015).

These equity principles originated while interpreting the equal protection clause of the federal constitution (Koski and Hahnel 2015). Berne and Steifel (1984) have provided other multiple definitions of equity in school finance and their measurement approach (Springer et al. 2015; Odden and Picus 2013; Hanushek and Lindseth 2009; West and Peterson 2007; Ladd et al. 1999; Downes and Stiefel 2015). Several studies have used these measures in estimating the impact of equity and adequacy lawsuits on reducing inequity in education funding across school districts (Corcoran and Evans 2015; Berry 2007; Murray et al. 1998).

Combining the liberal principles of horizontal equity and fiscal neutrality, the proponents of equality of educational opportunities sought judiciary's intervention in addressing school funding disparities. The school finance litigations forward the argument that the state should ensure the fundamental right of equal access to education for all and that the school finance structure should address the suspect classification based on property wealth per pupil (Odden and Picus 2013). Essentially, these proponents plead before the judiciary to issue directive to the federal and state governments for addressing fiscal disparities across school districts.

In 1971, the California Supreme Court's decision in *Serrano v. Priest* went in favor of these proponents. However, the proponents failed in their attempt to invoke federal constitution's Equal Protection Clause in the famous US Supreme Court's judgment in *Rodriguez v. San Antonio* in 1973 (Mickelson 2003; Chemerinsky 2003). Subsequently, proponents have sought recourse within the state legal system. Many subsequent judgments in different states have termed the funding inequity due to uneven local property-tax bases across school districts as unconstitutional. For example, the North Carolina Supreme Court's decision in the *Leandro v. the State of North Carolina* in 1997 termed the inadequate school funding to low-income communities as unconstitutional (Mickelson 2003). These education finance judgments have been very influential on the US public education after the federal Supreme Court ended segregation in schools in *Brown v. Board of Education* (Berry 2005).

In recent decades, the proponents of equity in education spending have turned to adequacy lawsuits after the Kentucky Supreme Court's ruling in the *Rose v. Council for Better Education* in 1989 that the state needed to take fiscal measure to ensure an adequate education (Baker 2018; Koski and Hahnel 2015; West and Peterson 2007). The argument under adequacy is that "spending on education must be adequate to provide all students with an education of the quality guaranteed by their state's constitution" (West and Peterson 2007, p. 5). The push for setting up of performance standards and accountability from the federal government has played a major role in the pursuit of adequacy lawsuits in particular (West and Peterson 2007) and school finance and policy in general (Gordon 2015). Proponents have used proficiency standards to calculate adequate cost of educating a child (West and Peterson 2007; Duncombe and Yinger 2015).

There are several opposing voices against the equity and adequacy lawsuits in education finance. Some experts argue that an adequate education cannot be achieved simply through fiscal equity (West and Peterson 2007). The meaning of adequacy varies from state to state (Springer et al. 2015). Hanushek, for example, argues that costing studies in adequate school finance in response to the state performance standards and accountability systems are theoretically and methodologically wrong (Hanushek 2005a, 2005b, 2006). In a recent study, Baker (2018) has undertaken careful and undisputable analysis to debunk these arguments.

The proponents of state finance equity litigations tasted both initial success and failure within a short duration of time. The California Supreme Court's decision in *Serrano v. Priest* went in favor of these proponents in 1971 (West and Peterson 2007; Springer et al. 2015). In 1976, the California Supreme Court reaffirmed its earlier judgment in *Serrano II*. At the federal level, the proponents tried to invoke federal constitution's Equal Protection Clause in addition to equity arguments in the famous US Supreme Court's judgment in *Rodriguez v. San Antonio* in 1973. However, the proponents did not succeed in this attempt (Mickelson 2003; Chemerinsky 2003; Springer et al. 2015). The federal Supreme Court disagreed with the argument that poor children in poor districts formed a suspect classification and that education was a fundamental right under the federal equal protection clause (Koski and Hahnel 2015). Instead, the Supreme Court applied the concept of rational relationship test in evaluating the Texas school finance system (Koski and Hahnel 2015). The Supreme Court ruled that the unequal spending across school districts did not violate the state's rational interest in maintaining local control over public education.

Subsequent to the legal debacle in the *Rodriguez* case, the proponents of funding equity had to change their legal strategies for seeking courts' intervention (Mickelson 2003). These proponents and the plaintiffs on their behalf based their cases on how the state constitutions and relevant legislations treated the issue of public education in order to seek legal recourse within the state court system (Mickelson 2003; West and Peterson 2007). The lawsuits have sought state courts' intervention in specifically defining and enlarging the constitutional treatment of public education with regard to equity in its provisioning (West and Peterson 2007).

These strategies have worked because the subsequent judgments have termed the local property-tax base dependent funding inequity across school districts as unconstitutional. The origin of these legal strategies is in New

Jersey Supreme Court's judgment in *Robinson v. Cahill* in 1973 (Koski and Hahnel 2015). The proponents, in this case, used the state constitutional article on education and constitutional equity provision in successfully arguing for equity in education spending. Since then, the state courts have interpreted the constitutional wordings including "thorough and efficient," "thorough and uniform," "general and uniform," and "support and maintenance of an efficient system of public free schools" in deciding on school finance litigations (Odden and Picus 2000, p. 36).

For example, the North Carolina Supreme Court's decision in the *Leandro v. the State of North Carolina* in 1997 (*Leandro I*) termed the inadequate school funding to low-income communities as unconstitutional (Corcoran and Evans 2015; Mickelson 2003). Overturning the trial court's ruling, the North Carolina Court of Appeal noted that the state had the obligation to prepare students to compete and partake in the society where they live (Almeida 2004). However, the Supreme Court did not direct the state to equalize funding across districts. Relying on the structural argument in the state constitution that local governments may use local revenues to supplement their local schools, the Supreme Court turned down plaintiff's equal protection claim. Similarly, in the *Abbott v. Burke* case in 1990 (*Abbott I*), the New Jersey Supreme Court directed the state to substantially equalize the public education funding between the poorer urban school districts and the wealthier school districts in order to protect the constitutional guarantee of inclusive and quality public education (Mickelson 2003). Other notable judgments going in favor of the proponents of equity in education finance are *Richland County v. Campbell*, South Carolina (1988); *Miliken v. Green*, Michigan (1973); *Abbott v. Burke II & III*, New Jersey (1990, 1994) (Corcoran and Evans 2015). In *Abbott II*, the New Jersey ordered the state to not only equalize the spending levels between property-rich and property-poor districts but to provide additional funding for meeting special needs of students, that is, ensure vertical equity.

There have been failures as well. For example, in 1987, in *Britt v. North Carolina Board of Education*, the North Carolina Supreme Court held that state constitution's education clause of "general and uniform system of free public schools" does not require the state to "provide identical opportunities to each and every student" (Almeida 2004, pp. 528–529). Between 1973 and 1989, equity lawsuits succeeded in eight cases and failed in fifteen (Ryan and Saunders 2004).

The movement to ensure equity in education financing under the legal mechanism slowed down subsequently (West and Peterson 2007). The implementation of judgments was slow due to political challenge. Also, while ensuring equity across districts, the aggregate spending on education fell. Plaintiffs lost equity cases in many states (Corcoran and Evans 2015; Hanushek and Lindseth 2009).

However, in recent decades, the movement for funding equity through judiciary's role has gained steam. The proponents have included the concept of adequacy of school financing in their recent legal pursuits. One of the rationales behind adequacy is to compel state legislatures to adopt and implement more equitable funding formulas (Baker 2018; Hanushek and Lindseth 2009). The argument under adequacy is that "spending on education must be adequate to provide all students with an education of the quality guaranteed by their state's constitution" (West and Peterson 2007, p. 5). The adequacy of education financing is a more expansive concept than equity, though it varies from state to state based on the language in state's constitution or legislation (West and Peterson 2007; Springer et al. 2015). For example, the adequacy of education financing implies that "states increase their overall spending, that they spend more on districts with student populations considered more expensive to educate, or that they do both" (West and Peterson 2007, p. 9). According to Koski and Hahnel (2015), adequacy concept requires setting standards for educational outcomes so that adequate funding levels could be calculated to achieve those standards. This concept does not compare across students in regard to educational resources or outcomes. However, it does specify some minimal level of school finance for all students. Many states have set academic performance standards that students in each school district are expected to achieve (Downes and Stiefel 2015). By inverting the production function of education to get adequate costing function, many studies have produced theoretical, methodological, and empirical guidelines for adequate school finance (Duncombe and Yinger 2015; Hanushek 2007b).

The push for setting up of educational performance standards and accountability at the behest of the federal government has also played a major role in the pursuit of adequacy lawsuits, in particular, (West and Peterson 2007) and school finance and policy, in general (Gordon 2015). The federal government has influenced school finance and policy in several other ways. Although in *Brown v. Board of Education*, the US Supreme Court ended school segregation in 1954, the southern states visibly started desegregating only after the passage of the Civil Rights Act of 1964. This act dismantled the Jim Crow doctrine of "separate but equal" treatment of African Americans in schools, public transportation, and other public places and services. In the subsequent year, the US Congress enacted ESEA of 1965 to provide compensatory Title I funds to school districts based on child poverty. Title I required Special programs for poor and "educationally disadvantaged" children. Title VI of the civil rights act required that federal funds be denied to public agencies not complying with the provisions of the act. Sufficient funds under Title I of the ESEA made Title VI of Civil rights act more effective (Gordon 2015). The reauthorizations of ESEA in Improving America's Schools Act, 1994, and the No Child Left Behind Act, 2001, include federal government's support and concern for the standard-based reforms. In the aftermath of the publication of *A Nation at Risk* in 1983, many states adopted accountability and standard-based reforms to address deficiencies in their schools as highlighted by the report. The 1994 legislation urged the states to establish minimum performance standards for students and schools along with mechanisms for ensuring accountability. NCLB emphasizes these standards and accountability more stringently.

The standards for gauging students' academic performance have enabled the judges to compare constitutional treatment of education against the performance norms set by the state. For example, Koski and Hahnel (2015, p. 49) note that "many judges are citing as evidence of educational inadequacy the failure of students to reach proficiency on state-mandated tests." The turning point in adequacy lawsuits was the Kentucky Supreme Court's ruling in the *Rose v. Council for Better Education* in 1989 that the state should take fiscal measure to ensure adequate education (Koski and Hahnel 2015; West and Peterson 2007). The Kentucky Supreme Court directed the state to provide adequate education that inculcated seven capabilities in students. For example, one of the capabilities the students should have is sufficient oral and written communication skills to survive in complex and dynamic society (Koski and Hahnel 2015).

Leandro II is another example in the tradition of adequacy lawsuit (Almeida 2004). *Leandro II* also refers to *Hoke County Board of Education v. State* (Almeida 2004). This lawsuit, however, also includes concerns with regard to vertical equity (Ryan and Saunders 2004). The trial in *Leandro II* began in 1999 after the Supreme Court constituted a trial court in remand under Judge Howard E. Manning, Jr. (Almeida 2004). The trial court rearranged the original adequacy litigation on remand in 2001 to include concerns with regard to at-risk students, such as students with poor background, poor health, unstable family, and low parental education (Ryan and Saunders 2004). One specific concern in *Leandro II* has been the need for pre-kindergarten program for poor children so that the goal of "sound basic education" is met (Almeida 2004, p. 535). This is because research has shown that more than half of achievement gaps at the end of twelfth grade between African American and white students can be eliminated if these two groups of students started kindergarten at same learning levels (Farkas 2003; Yeung and Pfeiffer 2009; Fryer and Levitt 2004). The trial court delivered final judgment in 2002 (Almeida 2004). The court required the state to provide an adequate education that conforms to minimum level of academic performance at or above grade level as defined in state's performance standards (Almeida 2004). In terms of vertical equity, the trial court also ruled that at-risk children are being denied constitutionally guaranteed right to receive the equal opportunity to a sound basic education (Almeida 2004). Judge Manning held that "the State bears the ultimate responsibility of ensuring that all school districts provide these resources to their at-risk children" (Almeida 2004, p. 541). The resources include smaller class size, providing tutoring, competent teachers and principals. However, the trial court did not explicitly direct the State to address these inequities through its budgets. This decision was challenged, but the Supreme Court reaffirmed the trial court's decision. Currently, the trial court in remand has the mandate to ensure that the state takes remedial steps so that the education system is in compliance with the constitution.[1]

As of 2018, out of the forty-six adequacy lawsuits in the United States the state courts ruled twenty-seven as unconstitutional.[2] According to Berry (2007), these education finance judgments have been very influential in the US public education after the federal Supreme Court ended segregation in schools in *Brown v. Board of Education*. Many scholars have investigated the impact of equity and adequacy judgments on school finance to see the movement toward the goal of equity (Baker 2018; Corcoran and Evans 2015; Berry 2007; Murray et al. 1998; Springer et al. 2006; Hoxby 2001). Building on the data and methodologies employed in Murray et al. (1998) and Harris et al. (2001), Corcoran and Evans (2015) find that court-mandated finance reforms have increased overall expenditures and reduced disparities between districts to a significantly higher extent than those states not subject to equity and adequacy lawsuits. Furthermore, two-thirds of the funding inequity across school district is explained by between-state differences in per-pupil spending (Corcoran and Evans 2015). Following a different measurement and methodological approach, Berry (2007) also finds significant impact of school finance judgments on school finance outcomes.

There are advantages and disadvantages of adequacy-based school finance reform. The adequacy concept rules out the constitutional dilemma of getting rid of local control in attaining funding equity. It also avoids opposition from political and economic elite (Koski and Hahnel 2015). Rich communities can continue to provide more than minimum required funding to attain a given level of performance standard (Minorini and Sugarman 1999; Koski and Hahnel 2015). The adequate education accommodates special needs (Minorini and Sugarman 1999). In *Leandro II*, the court ruled that the state had the obligation to do more for children from deprived backgrounds. The language of the education clause of a state constitution eases the interpretation of adequate education by courts. In the US cultural context, the general public is more tolerant toward economic and social inequality as long as they believe that every child has access to minimally adequate education to attain economic and social success (Koski and Hahnel 2015). Also, the concept of adequacy is lot clearer than various equity concepts. The state legislatures would just define an adequate education and set aside performance standards, conditions, and money for the local districts to implement such a public education (Koski and Hahnel 2015).

In reality, however, there is ambiguity in state constitutions about an adequate education. The legislatures and courts, therefore, do not have clear guidelines for interpretation. There is lack of agreement on goals of public education (Koski and Hahnel 2015). Researchers have usually measured educational outcome as student academic achievement or earnings. Grubb (2009) has suggested measuring educational outcomes in a dynamic sense. This dynamic measure includes, for example, resources that students bring to the school. There are practical difficulties in determining the composition of resources for desired outcomes vis-à-vis various background characteristics of students, including, for example, linguistic and economic (Koski and Hahnel 2015).

CRITIQUES AND ALTERNATIVE POLICY PRESCRIPTIONS FROM OPPONENTS

The critiques from the opponents of the pursuit of equity in education finance through adequacy lawsuits are directed toward the substantive interpretation of adequacy, the role of judiciary, the methods of calculating adequate finance and efficiency. One general comment is that the judiciary is encroaching the turf traditionally reserved as a legislative responsibility (Hanushek 2006; Hanushek and Lindseth 2009; West and Peterson 2007). Critics argue that an adequate education cannot be achieved simply through fiscal equity. They emphasize that there is no guarantee that the additional money provided to the schools will benefit students (West and Peterson 2007). The reason they provide is that courts do not have the expertise to ensure that new funds are spent productively. They further argue that the meaning of adequacy varies from state to state depending on the constitutional clause on education (Springer et al. 2015). According to these critics, adequacy is the least well-defined concept and is not linked to any particular guiding legal principle, and judges have to come up with an operational definition from the ambiguity of the educational clauses of the state constitutions (Baker and Green 2015).

Furthermore, critics argue that there are problems with costing studies in adequate school finance. These studies have originated in response to the performance standards that are set in the state accountability systems (Baker 2018; Duncombe et al. 1996; Duncombe and Yinger 1999, 2015). There are four methods of calculating the cost of public education under adequate educational opportunity principle (Downes and Stiefel 2015; Springer et al. 2015; Hanushek 2007a): (1) the econometric or cost function approach, (2) the successful schools or empirical approach, (3) the state-of-the-art or research-based approach, and (4) the professional judgment approach. All these methods involve two steps. First, the researchers establish the funding level commensurate with student performance requirements for at least one benchmark district. In the next step, researchers make adjustments for cost differentials in a district in relation to the benchmark district(s) (Imazeki and Reschovsky 2006; Duncombe 2002; Downes and Stiefel 2015). The general drawbacks (Downes and Stiefel 2015) of all these costing techniques are as follows: (1) these methods require high-quality data; (2) there is no widely accepted cost index measure for efficiency; and (3) the theory does not specify a single functional form. Hanushek (2005a, 2005b, 2007b) has questioned the costing studies on a more fundamental level. According to him, the existing methodologies are inadequate and they render any adequacy calculation meaningless. Some studies argue that because of the unreliable methods employed in extant costing studies, the legal process is susceptible to political influence (Springer and Guthrie 2007; Hanushek 2006). Hanushek and Lindseth (2009) further add that political interests of plaintiffs and teacher unions have interfered with the legal process. This argument applies to critics as well.

These critics believe that rather than more money, the efficiency in the use of money is important. According to them, the adequacy lawsuits ignore this tradeoff (Podgrusky 2007; Hanushek 2006; Hanushek and Lindseth 2009; Peterson 2010). They argue that from the resource side, the most expensive component is teacher and adequacy lawsuits entail more pay for recruiting and retaining teachers. However, there is no evidence that teachers are underpaid in public schools (Podgrusky 2007). This argument is misleading as Baker (2018) shows that teacher wages are noncompetitive in comparison to non-teacher wages. Increased spending on reducing class size is not beneficial to poor and minority students (Hanushek and Lindseth 2009), Baker (2018) agues and shows evidence to the contrary. There is little support for a positive effect of court-mandated school finance allocation on student achievement (Hanushek 2006). This argument does not take into account the tangible changes in allocation of resources post court decisions, and when this aspect is taken into account, the court-mandated school finance does have significant effect on student achievement (Baker 2018). Another critical argument is that rising funding equity has no relation to equity in labor market outcomes for the students (Hanushek and Somers 2001). However, recent studies using Tennessee STARR project data and applying rigorous analytical technique to find that funding equity does promote equitable life outcomes (Baker 2018).

Opponents have prescribed alternative policy reforms based on strong performance-based accountability system (Hanushek 2006). Hanushek and Lindseth (2009) also refer to this policy option as "performance-based funding system." Figlio and Ladd (2015) have summarized elements of education policy reform under the school-based accountability system. This system sets student performance standards and requires the schools to allocate resources to achieve those standards. Furthermore, the schools need to institute an incentive system for rewarding good performing teachers and administrators and punishing incompetent ones. The incentive system includes pay for performance and changes in teacher tenure rules. In essence, the accountability system is aimed at addressing the principal–agent problem (Figlio and Ladd 2015). The growth models would measure performances of teachers by comparing the actual student achievements against the set standards. Another element of this reformed system is the widening of choices for parents in the form of vouchers and charter schools. The broader view in school choice options is that the market-like competition would nudge the public schools toward efficiency in resource use and better educational outcomes. There should be transparency in resource use and allocation on various programs. This transparency in the processes in respect of the origin of resources, individual school-wise allocation, details on teachers and their allocation across schools is critical in informed decision making.

The performance and accountability system of public education has several drawbacks as well. The measures of performance do not take into account efficiency in resource use by the school rather rank schools on gains in their students' achievement (Figlio and Ladd 2015). Performance-based reward system ignores the reality that some schools may lack sufficient resources to attain proficiency standards. Also, schools tend to concentrate their resources on grades and subjects that are tested for performance growth (Figlio 2006; Ladd and Zelli 2002; Deere and Strayer 2001). Teachers and schools also narrow down curriculum and instructional focus from nontested to tested subjects (Hamilton et al. 2005; Koretz and Hamilton 2006; Linn 2000; Stecher et al. 2000). The overall effect of accountability-based public school system on student achievement is modest at best (Figlio and Ladd 2008; Lee 2006; Hanushek and Raymond 2005; Carony and Loeb 2002).

STUDENT, FAMILY, SCHOOL, AND SOCIETAL-LEVEL FACTORS

The adequacy-based school system does not require schools to actually attain performance standards. Adequacy-based reform does not look into how the schools are allocating their resources and how those allocations are related to student outcomes. The performance-based accountability system, on the other hand, does require the schools to make progress toward specified performance standards. In establishing the (in-)efficacy of both types of school reforms, researchers have either shown whether money matters, how money matters.

I covered this argument in the previous chapter. However, both the adequacy and accountability-based reforms pay scant attention to nonschool environments that significantly influence student achievement (Condron 2009). The most prominently discussed nonschool factor is students' race and socioeconomic background. Family educational resources, child's health status, residential stability, and quality of housing explain achievement gaps between low SES and high SES students (Rothstein 2004). The low SES students include disproportionately high number of African Americans (Condron 2009).

The interest in the role of nonschool factors in achievement dates back to the Equality of Educational Opportunity study by Coleman and his colleagues (Coleman et al. 1966). The often-cited finding of the study is that students' family background is far more influential in explaining the achievement gap than both within and between school factors. Coleman et al. (1966) concluded that school resources had negligible impact on student achievement. However, using the same data and contemporary HLM models, Borman and Dowling (2010) show that conclusions in Coleman et al. were wrong. School resources did explain two-fifth of the achievement gap. Some sociologists maintain the view that public policy cannot solve the achievement gaps problem as long as the broader structure of social stratification is one of the reason behind learning gaps and unless policies also address the factors behind social stratification (Anyon 2005; Kozol 1992; Mickelson 2003; Wilson 1998; Rothstein 2004).

Socioeconomic status explains a very large portion (85% for math and 100% for reading) of black–white achievement gaps before students enter school (Fryer and Levitt 2005). Using different datasets, others show much lower effects of 25 percent to 40 percent (Murnane et al. 2006). Studies show that more than half of the black–white achievement gaps at the end of the twelfth grade could be eliminated if achievement gaps before children enter school is eliminated (Farkas 2003; Yeung and Pfeiffer 2009; Fryer and Levitt 2004).

Both within and between school factors play important roles in maintaining social stratification in achievement. Fryer and Levitt (2005) show that achievements gaps grow within schools net of other predictors. Hanushek and Rivkin (2006), on the other hand, show that between school factors explain the gaps. Reardon (2007) situates this confusion in decomposing achievement gaps into between and within school categories. From the public policy perspective, some of the within school factors that have bearing on student achievement are ability grouping, tracking, teacher expectations, and class size (Oakes 1985, 1990; Farkas 2003, Mickelson 2003). Student achievement gaps between African American and white students and between higher and lower SES students within schools are partly attributable to teachers' biases favoring middle-class students and to schools' greater reliance on curriculum differentiation through the use of academic and nonacademic tracking (Borman and Dowling 2010).

The two important between school factors related to student achievement gaps are racial segregation and teacher quality. Resegregation is on the rise in the United States (Orfield and Yun 1999). Racially diverse peers positively influence students' academic learning in the short and long runs (Mickelson 2001; Cooley 2009). Moreover, having diverse peers is favorable to lowest-performing nonwhites (Cooley 2009). Having high achieving peers is helpful to low performing students, but having low performing students does not benefit the high achievers (Hoxby and Weingrath 2005). Teacher quality does matter in student performance, and qualified teachers are unequally distributed across schools (Jackson 2009; Boyd et al. 2005). Also, experienced and qualified teachers sort themselves disproportionately to suburban schools.

All the inequalities in nonschool and school factors mirror the socio-economic structure of the larger society. Schools simply reproduce them (Mickelson 2003). Roscigno et al. (2006) argue that resources that influence educational outcomes are tied to the economic opportunity structure of the region and vary across inner city, rural, and suburban places. They show that inner-city and rural areas have disadvantages in both family and school resources. These resource inequalities influence educational investments at family and school levels which in turn significantly influence academic achievement (Roscigno et al. 2006).

In the larger socioeconomic environment of a metropolitan area, lower-income population remains segregated in inner city. This population dispro-portionately comprises African Americans (Wilson 1987; Jargowsky 1997). There is spatial mismatch in the labor market. This spatial mismatch implies that new jobs are being created in largely white suburbs, but the blacks are residentially concentrated in the inner city because of segregation in the housing market. Blacks face joblessness, lower wages, and longer commutes to work (Kain 1968; Ihlanfeldt and Sjoquist 1998). Spatial mismatch adds to higher unemployment rates among central city minorities. Lower education levels and employer discrimination further disadvantage residentially concentrated minorities (Preston and McLafferty 1999). Impediments to commuting, inadequate information about the jobs and feeling lack of acceptance among minorities at suburban job sites also influence job access (Ihlanfeldt and Sjoquist 1998). Suburban zoning practices discourage low-income families in moving into those locations (Holzer 1991). The tax incentives for owner-occupied housing and the public investment in transportation infrastructure disproportionately aid the high-income group in choosing suburbresidential location (Voith 2000). "Eliminating housing and job dis-crimination and significantly improving the job skills of minority workers are the long-run solutions to unequal geographic opportunity within metropolitan areas" (Ihlanfeldt and Sjoquist 1998, p. 886). Pointing to discriminatory preferences of landlords, rental agents, or residents in residential segregation, Raphael and Stoll (2010) suggest multipronged policies for removing housing market flaws.

Jonathan Kozol in his works (1967 & 1992) brought attention to the pathetic teaching conditions in inner-city schools. This geographic and economic reality is not very different from the residential and job market discrimination in the regional context. This is why exploration of educational processes is important. This is why researchers should look into the internal workings of schools and school systems and urban environment to explain disparities in educational outcomes (Ladd et al. 1999; Mickelson 2003; Grubb 2009; Condron 2009; Roza 2010).

CONCLUDING REMARKS

In spite of numerous educational reform policies, disparities in school resources and educational outcomes have persisted, although at a lesser degree than before (Baker 2018). State governments have tried to reduce inequity in education finance through different funding formulas. The local control for funding and provisioning of public education and flaws in different funding formulas are the chief reasons in funding disparity. In recent decades, proponents of funding equity have successfully used the state judicial system through equity and adequacy lawsuits to reduce intrastate funding inequity. However, funding disparities across school districts have not disappeared. The adequacy lawsuits are not in conflict with funding disparity if the state governments ensure minimal level of funding in each school district for providing quality education as per state performance standards. Adequacy compliant school finance reform also makes room for programs for special needs students.

However, opponents of adequacy-based school finance reform have suggested an alternate public education reform based on performance standards and accountability. These opponents have argued that judiciary is encroaching on legislature's turf through reforms suggested in judgments on adequacy litigations. According to this view, judges are not in a position to ascertain the magnitude and the allocation of resources commensurate with performance standards. Also, the adequacy-based school reform does not require that additional money should improve educational outcomes. While emphasizing that additional money does not matter in educational outcomes, these opponents have suggested that schools and teachers should be held accountable against performance standards. This performance-based funding should reward performance and punish ineffective teachers, schools, and leaders. Furthermore, parents should have more choice over selection of schools. There should be transparency in fund allocation, information about teachers, distribution of teachers and other resources across schools.

However, the measures of performance do not take into account efficiency in resource use by the schools. They rank schools on gains in their students' achievement. Performance-based reward system also ignores the fact that some schools may lack sufficient resources to attain proficiency standards. Schools also tend to concentrate their resources on grades and subjects that are tested for performance growth. Teachers and schools also narrow down curriculum and instructional focus from nontested to tested subjects. Also, the overall effect of accountability-based public school system on student achievement is modest at best.

Both the adequacy and accountability-based reforms pay inadequate attention to nonschool environments that significantly influence student achievement. The inequalities in nonschool and school factors mirror the socioeconomic structure of the larger society. Schools simply reproduce them. Socioeconomic status explains a large variation in achievement gaps. Both family and school resources are distributed unevenly across regions. Low income and minority families are disproportionately concentrated in inner cities. There are widespread discrimination and mismatch in the job and housing market in metropolitan regions. More qualified teachers sort themselves to rich and high performing suburban schools. Inner-city schools are segregated with minority and low-income students. Within schools, there is inequity in distribution of track placement, curriculum, and teacher's expectations.

As long as the broader structure of social stratification is one of the reasons behind learning gaps, public policy cannot solve this problem without appropriately addressing the factors behind social, geographic, and economic stratification. The discriminatory processes in schools mirror these societal environments. This is why exploration of educational processes is important. Researchers look into the internal workings of schools and school systems to explain disparities in educational outcomes. Public policies on housing, poverty, health, employment, economic development, and education have to strike a coherent balance in addressing student achievement gaps.

NOTES

1. *Leandro II – Hoke County Bd. of Educ. v. State* 599 S.E.2d 365 (N.C. 2004).
2. See http://schoolfunding.info/litigation-map/ (accessed 02/06/2019).

Chapter 3

The Ubiquitous School Choice in Public Education and Local Political Leadership in the United States

In most countries around the world, governments at various levels are responsible for providing collective goods and services. In general, any study of public policy is concerned with one or more aspects of provisioning of public goods. The fiscal policy of governments at different levels is concerned with raising money to pay for the cost of public programs for the delivery of collective goods and services. In the United States, there is a three-tier government system for providing public goods: federal, state, and local governments. At the local level, there are both general-purpose and single-purpose local governments. For example, municipalities provide a range of public services, such as trash collection, police, and transit, while local school districts provide only public education. Economic theory does not strictly consider public education a classical public good because private market can also provide schools. However, in most societies across the globe, school education is mainly in the domain of public sector (Fischel 2009). Therefore, from the modern social and political standpoint, formal education is effectively a public good.

The issues of allocative and productive efficiency of provision and equity of distribution are of paramount importance in case of most public goods, including public education. Prior to the seminal work by Charles Tiebout in 1956, the scholars of public finance, such as Richard A. Musgrave and Paul A. Samuelson, believed that the optimal level of expenditure on public goods is indeterminate and that the national income allocated on providing such goods is nonoptimal when compared to the allocation on private goods (Musgrave 1939; Samuelson 1954). However, Tiebout's paper, "A Pure Theory of Local Expenditures," successfully challenged this view and argued that the "market failure" in the provision of public good in case of the national government need not apply in case of the local governments. Specifically, Tiebout argued that the preferences of residents in the local government jurisdiction can be captured more adequately than at the national level and the solution for the level of local expenditure on public goods can be found. Ostrom et al. (1961) further expanded Tiebout's model of local public finance. This extended work not only emphasized the virtues of fragmented governments in a metropolitan area, it also argued against a single metropolitan-wide government system. In the last five decades, the debate over the relative merits and demerits of centralized v. decentralized forms of local governments in general has continued. This debate is also applicable in case of the single-purpose school districts.

In this chapter, I bring together the literature that argues both for the centralization and decentralization of local government, in general, and school district, in particular. I have organized the chapter into several sections. In section 1, I summarize the key arguments in this regard. I also explain the conceptual distinction between allocative and productive efficiency. In section 2, I bring together the empirical literature on debate over centralized v. decentralized form of local governments including school districts. I conclude in section 3.

CONSOLIDATION V. FRAGMENTATION: GENERAL LOCAL GOVERNMENTS AND SCHOOL DISTRICTS

The debate over the relative merits and demerits of centralized metropolitan government vis-à-vis decentralized local governments in the metropolitan area has hinged on principles of equity, local control, allocative efficiency, and productive efficiency. The concepts and terms, such as the characteristics of public goods, distinction between production and provision, spillovers, poverty, racial and socioeconomic segregation, urban sprawl and cooperation among local governments, also figure in the major arguments of this debate. Howell-Moroney (2008) and Jimenez and Hendrick (2010) have critically synthesized the two sides of the debate over appropriate forms of local governments in the metropolitan area.

The proponents of decentralization or fragmentation argue for the existence of numerous local governments in the metropolitan area (Ostrom et al. 1961). This is necessary to accommodate heterogeneity in individual preferences for optimal tax–expenditure bundle of public goods. Lyons and Lowery (1989, p. 533) note that the polycentric model of local government "focuses on the need to maintain numerous units of local governments in each urban area in order to maximize opportunities for individual citizens to choose a tax-service package that best suits their needs."

The polycentric local governments also work against the natural tendency of governments to extract higher taxes from residents (Brennan and

Buchanan 1980; Jimenez and Hendrick 2010). This tendency of governments is also termed as Leviathan behavior (Brennan and Buchanan 1980; Craw 2008). Specifically, more decentralized local governments in metropolitan region leads to economy in government spending and taxation. The central concern in the literature on Leviathan model is in estimating the relationship between levels of interjurisdictional competition and levels of taxation and spending. This correspondence is also termed as monopoly power of local governments (Craw 2008). Consistent with public-choice and Leviathan models, proponents of reformism hypothesis argue that type of local government also matters in controlling inflated public budgets and inefficiencies in local taxation and spending (Craw 2008; Frant 1996; Feiock et al. 2003). The reformists argue that council–manager form of local government and at-large council elections are better than the mayor–council government and ward-based council elections in this regard.

The public-choice model pioneered by Tiebout in 1956 captures the major arguments for fragmentation. This theory is concerned with the choice of efficient levels of goods and services made by the residents within a local jurisdiction (Craw 2008; Howell-Moroney 2008; Jimenez and Hendrick 2010). In essence, the public-choice theory posits that individuals choose to live in a local political jurisdiction with a mixture of tax–expenditure bundle that matches their preferences and budgets (Harris et al. 2001; Poterba 1997). The communities at the local level also seek to attain optimum size for the efficient delivery of public goods and service by local governments. The pursuit of optimum size is essential in order to lower the average cost of public goods and services. The residents reveal their preferences by choosing a package of public goods and services offered by local governments. If the public goods and services are offered efficiently at some optimum size, the migration of the residents will occur until that optimum size has been reached. By choosing to reside in a community having a package of public goods and services, the resident reveals his preferences or willingness to pay, and the local government can tax the community in order to sustain the level of public goods.

This simultaneous occurrence of the matching of residents' preferences and attaining optimum size of the local community ensures both allocative and productive efficiency in the delivery of public goods at the local level. According to Jimenez and Hendrick (2010), allocative efficiency entails matching of demand for, and supply of, public goods. The productive efficiency or the technical efficiency connotes lower average cost of producing and providing a given level of public good. In the words of the authors:

> Allocative efficiency is about government responsiveness, that is, the extent to which government supplies the goods and services preferred by local residents. Technical efficiency, on the other hand, involves producing a higher level of

output given the same level of input, thereby reducing the cost of public services. (Jimenez and Hendrick 2010, p. 259)

In case of the single-purpose school districts, Hoxby (1994, 1999) has provided similar explanations of allocative and productive efficiencies. Hoxby
(1994) argues that residents move to another school district in case the
marginal benefit of school spending is not aligned with its marginal cost in
residents' school district. Because of this Tiebout process, property tax-based
school finance achieves a high level of allocative efficiency. With regard
to productive efficiency or productivity, Hoxby (1999) emphasizes the link
between consolidated or fragmented structure of school districts and economy in providing public schools. Hoxby (1999) favors decentralized form of
school districts on this count.

The public-choice model of fragmented local governments has argued
that the residents within such community are better informed and are more
knowledgeable about the level of public services and tax incidence. Hence,
their participation in the governance is more, and they tend to be more satisfied with public services. In contrast, the public-choice theorists also argue
that the citizens in the consolidated governance systems are less informed and
less knowledgeable about the combination of tax-service package provided
by the local government (Lyons and Lowery 1989). Because the size of the
local government is large, the citizens find themselves unable to influence the
decisions made by the local government. The residents also participate less in
the governance process and are more likely to be dissatisfied with the services
and performance of their governments.

The proponents of centralized local government in an urban area argue
against fragmented local governments on both efficiency and equity grounds.
These scholars show a concern about the spillovers existing in the fragmented governments. The argument is that the "polycentric" governments
cause spillover problems and hence the solution suggested may no longer be
efficient. Howell-Moroney (2008) has brought such concerns with the central
assumptions in the public-choice model of fragmented local governments and
the ground realities in which such polycentric governments work. He cites
some recent studies and notes that "the residential segregation of people by
race and class and the many costs of sprawl are magnified and augmented
by arrangements that defer to multiple local jurisdictions" (Howell-Moroney
2008, p. 100). These spillovers lead to price distortions and people do not pay
true costs associated with a polycentric institutional arrangement. In this way,
the preferences of the residents are not truly captured by the local governments for optimum tax-service package.

Scholars have also argued against decentralized model of local governments on equity grounds. For example, Lyons and Lowery (1989) argue that

any inequity in spending on public goods among the local governments is acceptable on the efficiency criteria under the public-choice model, because the residents made a conscious decision to live in communities with suitable tax–expenditure offerings. Subsequently, the problems of sprawl and concentrated poverty are largely due to the existence of municipal boundaries that "circumscribe notions of collective responsibility" (Howell-Moroney 2008, p. 98). Centralized local governments can overcome these inequalities by fairly distributing the costs of providing public services (Lineberry 1970).

These criticisms have brought the polycentric theory of local governments to the initial point from where Tiebout's seminal work began. The free rider problem and spillover effects are well-accepted phenomena associated with the provision of public goods and services at higher levels of governments. These phenomena make the provisioning of public goods inefficient, that is, there is no "market-type" solution. According to Howell-Moroney (2008), the important arguments that highlight the problem associated with spillover are:

- The urban sprawl has many associated costs that are often borne by other communities in the same metropolitan area.
- The impacts of race and class-based segregation are also spillovers resulting from the drain of resources from central city areas.
- Cross-municipal subsidization of infrastructure is another type of spillover.
- There are environment impacts from sprawl, including air pollution from high automobile use associated with low-density sprawl in American cities.

The proponents of consolidation of local governments strongly argue that the spillovers are occurring "within" the metropolitan area. This essentially means that the fragmented local governments are not able to capture costs arising due to polycentric nature of institutional arrangements within the metropolitan areas. Therefore, centralized local governments are well suited to capture these spillovers and costs due to sprawl (Lyons and Lowery 1989; Howell-Moroney 2008, Jimenez and Hendrick 2010).

Proponents of decentralized local governments have defended against the critiques advanced by proponents of centralized local governments. They have argued that there are a number of options available to the local governments for public service delivery to the citizens (Ostrom et al. 1961; ACIR 1987). It involves a number of arrangements between the resident, the local government, private sector, and another local government. As regards the production of the goods and services in question, the local governments have a number of options too. They can produce by themselves, engage private sector through contract and contract with other local governments producing that good, or undertake joint production.

Two points are worth noting in this regard. One is that the choice of provision of goods and services, that is, government is different from governance. Citizens vote their choices for the delivery of different kinds of goods and services. The government led by the elected officials then decides the best way to provide those goods and services. In this way, there is a correspondence between the local demand for public goods and local government spending. The main driver of this correspondence is the income level and tax price of the local median voter (Borcherding and Deacon 1972; Bergstrom and Goodman 1973; Ahmed and Greene 2000). This is what the public-choice literature terms as the median voter hypothesis.

Another point is that it is not necessary for the governments to produce goods and services by themselves. The difference between provision and production is what gives the local governments a range of options to provide goods and services to its residents (Howell-Moroney 2008). The various arrangements that can be made for the provisioning of different goods and services are: government service provision, intergovernmental arrangement, contracting with private sector, franchise, grant, voucher, private market, voluntary service, self-service, and government vending. These arrangements depend on the characteristics of the goods and services to be provided. In all of these arrangements, the originating flow of service and cost for such service vary.

According to Howell-Moroney (2008), this distinction between public service provision and production has allowed the proponents of public choice to distinguish between metropolitan government and governance. Specifically, proponents of decentralized local governments argue that differing scales of service provision in different contexts do not necessitate the existence of a metropolitan-wide Leviathan regional government. Interlocal cooperation in conjunction with other choices available to the local governments on account of differentiation between production and provision should suffice to produce and provide a particular service at larger scales (Miller 2002; Parks and Oakerson 1993, 2000; Stephens and Wikstrom 2000; McGinnis 1999; Wood 2005). Moreover, fragmented local governments entail greater local control and are commensurate with the basic constitutional principles of limited government and separation of power (Howell-Moroney 2008; Ostrom 1997).

In recent times, the fragmentation and consolidation debate has morphed into arguments for and against regionalism and localism (Jimenez and Hendrick 2010). The conceptual distinction between production and provision and between government and governance has moved the debate over two contrasting forms of local governments to metropolitan governance (Howel-Moroney 2008). The major arguments in the debate between regionalism and localism have not changed though. This debate is in response to challenges in solving problems that overlap many local political boundaries within a metropolitan region, such as urban sprawl, declining regional economies, environmental degradation, incoherent land use policy, inequities in housing, education and tax policy within the region (Foster 2001). In this light, regionalism generally means "ways of thinking and acting at the regional scale" (Foster 2001, p. 1). Specifically, regionalism "refer[s] to shifting authority and functions from local, state or national governments to regional entities" (Foster 2001, p. 7).

Regionalism has five forms, according to Foster (2001): a structure, programs and policies, partnerships and agreements, processes and practices, and cultural expressions. Foster (2001) provides an example for each of these forms. City–county consolidation is an example of structural regionalism. Regional fair-share housing policy is an example of regionalism in the form of programs and policies. Interlocal compact is manifestation of regionalism as partnerships and agreements. Regional forum is regionalism in the form of processes and practices. Finally, regional norms or logos are regionalism as cultural expressions.

The general conditions of economies of scale, spillover effect, need for cross-border cooperation, residents' preferences, need for standardization based on equity and threshold levels warrant regionalism. Foster (2001) argues that metropolitan areas have the scale to address problems in totality. Local governments cannot address them in isolation. The complicated ills, such as urban sprawl and environment pollution, are spread over more than one locality. Therefore, only a coordinated effort on the part of the local governments can tailor solutions for such ills. Foster (2001) further argues that regional governance is more suitable when the goal is to achieve equity and environmental sustainability. The traditional reliance on local governments is preferable if the goal is to ensure political participation and accountability. With regard to efficiency and economic growth, the two systems of governance fare equally (Foster 2001). While evaluating the federal administration of housing and workforce policy, Hughes (2000) argues that these programs are fragmented and pose obstacles in regional cooperation. Instead, these programs could be better administered at the metropolitan level either through structural consolidation or functional consolidation.

Summers (2000) has emphasized the importance of externalities and optimum size of public service in regionalism. The author argues that even with redistribution of resources in the form of intergovernmental aid, the local jurisdiction bears significant costs associated with metropolitan-wide poverty-related programs, such as public welfare and hospitals, and other functions, such as police and education services. Voith (1998) has argued that suburbs do well in terms of housing values and family incomes if income in their central cities also rises. So the benefit from maintaining a healthy urban core percolates to peripheral urban communities as well. This externality supports the need for regionalism in metro areas. Summers (2000) also argues that certain services are less costly to provide if they serve certain threshold limit. For example, public transportation, solid waste disposal, centralized purchasing.

There are many factors to consider in deciding whether a service should be provided regionally or locally (Foster 2001). Services such as sewer and water, utilities, airports, highways, transit, and environment planning and management require economies of scale, large service area, narrow preferences, high level of cross-border cooperation, and standardization in delivery. These considerations entail regionalism in the provision of such services. However, services, such as police control, fire, community development, local planning and zoning, schools, parks, libraries, garbage collection, and so on are better suited to local provision, according to Foster (2001). This is because there is absence of economies of scale, no threshold is required, preferences are wide, little cross-border cooperation is required, and there is no need for standardization.

Local interaction between residents is also an important factor. Foster (2001) argues that residents of a metropolitan region come in contact with each other on regular basis. They share their place-related ideas, problems, and matters of significance for the metropolitan region. This interaction culminates in a broader sense of metropolitan community. Problems such as air pollution, transportation planning, employment, global competitiveness are viewed at the regional level. At the same time, services, such as police control, fire, and community development, are generally viewed locally. The bottom-line is: "As more frequent and durable cross-border links turn once local problems into metropolitan ones, regions gain significance" (Foster 2001, p. 4).

However, any regional action faces philosophical, political, governance, and empirical challenges, according to Foster (2001). Philosophically, it is imperative to safeguard individual freedom while trying to achieve larger common good. Regional action creates winners and losers. This creates political conflict. Normally, residents are more loyal to their local communities than the whole region. Regional action has to overcome this political challenge. Even after overcoming the above challenges, regions lack formal structure or authority to realize metropolitan public good. Lastly, there is lack of conclusive evidence in support of the positive impact of regionalism on economic development. This weakens the regionalism argument.

While implementing regional action, there are two important issues to consider. First, regionalism must conform to equivalence principle (Foster 2001). Second, Higgins and Savoie (1995) suggest that development planning and policy should be done at the level of smallest possible decision-making unit. The equivalence principle of governance implies that "the decision-making unit of a problem should equate to both its financing unit and the area affected" (Foster 2001, p. 4). The two principles imply that services aimed at solving problems that transcend local boundaries should come through regional action. In the absence of any spillover, the local provision is more suitable. The equivalence principle is consistent with the idea of economies of scale, equity, and standardization of services, because these issues have regional reach. Since regional problems involve more than one community, regional action makes sense with regard to bottom-up planning and policy approach suggested by Higgins and Savoie (1995). The authors have argued that "there are development activities which cannot be handled exclusively at the local level but which need not go to the national level. These are the proper concern of the regional authorities" (Higgins and Savoie 1995, p. 402).

Foster (2001) believes that public education is better provided locally because there is absence of scale economies, no threshold is required, preferences are wide, little cross-border cooperation is required, and there is no need for standardization. Berry and West (2010) hold the view that larger school districts may provide scale economies, but this consolidation gain does not compare against the forgone gains, such as stronger sense of belonging and opportunity for close relationships with teachers and administrators, from fragmented and smaller school districts. One study has pointed to the increase in opportunity costs for travel time for parents and students when several school districts consolidate (Kenney 1982). Also, consolidation of school districts may not produce economies of scale if there is no reduction in capital and administrative costs (Duncombe et al. 1995). However, several empirical studies support allocative and productive efficiency gains from consolidation of school districts (Andrews et al. 2002).

EMPIRICAL LITERATURE ON CENTRALIZATION AND DECENTRALIZATION DEBATE

In terms of productive efficiency, many studies have found the evidence that fragmentation leads to lower spending (Oakerson 1999; Boyne 1992a). But there are studies that did not support productive efficiency gain due to fragmentation. Proponents of fragmentation have criticized these studies for inaccurately measuring the governing structure or not recognizing the complexity of governing structure in many locales. For instance, some of the studies failed to standardize the measure of fragmentation by population (Stansel 2006; Dolan 1990). On the other hand, Boyne (1992b) has questioned Dolan's (1990) methodology for not standardizing the measure of fragmentation by taking into account the regional norms. Also, the fragmentation of general-purpose governments lowers spending, but fragmentation of special-purpose governments produces the opposite effect (Nelson 1986; Zax 1989; Stansel 2006; Berry 2008; Eberts and Gronberg 1988; Craw 2008; Schneider 1986, 1989). This is because multipurpose governments compete more by offering different bundles of services in comparison to single-purpose governments (Eberts and Gronberg 1988; Boyne 1992a; Stansel 2006; Foster 1997).

In terms of allocative efficiency, several studies have found that citizens of smaller jurisdictions show greater satisfaction with law enforcement compared to residents of bigger communities (Ostrom 1976; Ostrom and Smith 1976; Ostrom et al. 1978). However, DeHoog et al. (1990) contend that these studies only confirmed city size effects instead of fragmentation. Specifically, these studies compared large and small jurisdictions within the same metropolitan area thereby ruling out inferences about the impact of local governing structure. Using survey data from five matched pairs of neighborhoods in consolidated versus fragmented metropolitan areas in Kentucky, DeHoog et al. (1990) found that overall citizen satisfaction did not vary systematically between the two governmental structures. Study by Lyons and Lowery (1989) also pertains to the citizens' evaluation of the urban governments and the services they provide. Lyons and Lowery (1989), undertook citizen survey in two counties in Kentucky. The Louisville-Jefferson County has about 100 municipalities and hence can be considered a highly fragmented system of governments. In contrast, the Lexington-Fayette County is a consolidated county. The research findings of this book do not support the basic arguments contained in the public-choice theory. According to Lyons and Lowery (1989, p. 533),

> citizens living in smaller local jurisdictions located in the more fragmented system were not better informed about the scope and nature of their local tax-service package; they were not more efficacious about their relationships with their local governments; they were not more likely to participate in local affairs; and they were not more satisfied with their local services and the performance of their local governments than their counterparts living in the consolidated setting. Nor did the evidence support the public-choice contention that satisfaction with local services is more widely dispersed across local jurisdictions in more fragmented systems.

Several empirical studies report that government fragmentation leads to racial segregation (Morgan and Morescal 1999; Weiher 1991; Rusk 1993; Burns 1994; Altshuler et al. 1999). Segregation by race, income, and education from 1960 to 1980 occurred increasingly at the city level in comparison to the neighborhood level (Weiher 1991). The concern regarding urban sprawl has also been empirically evaluated. Analyzing a sample of 822 metropolitan counties, Caruthers (2003) finds that fragmentation of municipal and special district governments increased growth outside of incorporated areas. Also, fragmentation of general- and special-purpose governments had a two-pronged relationship with urban sprawl (Carruthers and Ulfarsson 2002). First, Tiebout process facilitated the formation of new communities in unincorporated areas. Next, new local governments came up to provide public services. However, Razin and Rosentraub's (2000) find that residential sprawl had significant positive effects on fragmentation, but fragmentation did not predict sprawl.

In respect of school districts, several studies have evaluated the productive efficiency of consolidated and fragmented governmental structures. But most studies have measured just the district size effects instead of the comparative effects of consolidation versus fragmentation. However, economies of scale effects of district size do make a case for consolidating smaller school districts. About three-and-a-half decades ago, Fox (1981) reviewed the literature on economies of size. Andrews et al. (2002) have reviewed the school size effects at class, school, and district levels. At the district level, there is significant and negative relationship between school district size and per-pupil expenditure, but there is a threshold limit in terms of student enrolments. Also, most of the studies did not take into account the increase in travel costs for parents and students in consolidated school districts (Andrews et al. 2002) as pointed out by Kenny (1982).

Gordon and Knight (2008) have studied the impact of whole-grade sharing and administrative consolidation of school districts induced by the state fiscal incentives in Iowa. They do not find support for efficiency gains from either whole-grade sharing or consolidation. Driscoll et al. (2003) report that district size negatively impacts educational achievement, and the worst effect is on middle school student performance. Berry and West (2010) find that larger districts provide modestly higher returns to education and increased educational achievement in most specifications, but any gains from the consolidation of districts do not compensate the harmful effects of larger schools.

Few studies have also evaluated the impact of competition among public school districts in a metropolitan area on student achievement. This is a very under-researched area (Gill and Booker 2015), and we take this up in the next chapter. Controlling for endogeneity, Hoxby (2000) found positive relationship between more competition and student achievement. However, Rothstein (2005) found that Hoxby's results did not hold across various specifications. Earlier, Hoxby (1994), extending the work by Borland and Howsen (1992), reported that metropolitan areas with many school districts are better for student performance. Hoxby (1994) concludes that Tiebout competition is better at addressing the allocative efficiency issue of assuring that public schooling is not underprovided. In terms of productive efficiency, Peltzman (1993, 1996) reported that more centralized school districts do not exhibit economies of scale. Hoxby (1994) also reports that metropolitan areas that are more in line with the Tiebout process are also more cost-effective.

CONCLUDING REMARKS

This chapter has reviewed the extant literature on the debate over consolidation and fragmentation of local governments. Over the last five-and-a-half decades, economic and political theories have successfully articulated that local governments are allocatively and productively superior to state and federal governments in providing most of the local public goods and services. However, scholars have vigorously debated over the appropriate form of the local government in the urban regional context. Proponents of fragmented local governments find theoretical and empirical support in terms of allocative and productive efficiencies. Proponents of centralized local governments contend that fragmented local governments cause spillovers, urban sprawl, and racial and economic segregation, and hence such governments are allocatively and productively inefficient. According to proponents of centralization, metropolitan-wide local government is both more equitable and efficient. Proponents of decentralization have acknowledged that provisioning of several public goods and services transcend local political boundaries. But they contend that in such specific situations, the local governments should take the call between production and provision and interlocal arrangements.

In recent times, the agreement over the overlap of a number of urban problems over several local boundaries has moved the rigid and dichotomous debate over fragmentation and consolidation to the debate over regionalism versus localism. The principles of fiscal and governance equivalence are the key teasers in this debate. Certain services entail economies of scale, large service area, narrow preferences, high level of cross-border cooperation, and standardization in delivery. These considerations necessitate regionalism in the provision of such services. Other services are better suited to local provision, because there is absence of economies of scale, no threshold is required, preferences are wide, little cross-border cooperation is required, and there is no need for standardization. Public education falls in the latter category, according to Foster (2001).

However, larger school districts may provide scale economies, but this consolidation gain does not compare against the forgone gains from fragmented and smaller school districts. There is a need to consider increase in opportunity costs for travel time for parents and students when several school districts consolidate. Also, consolidation of school districts may not produce economies of scale if there is no reduction in capital and administrative costs. Although several empirical studies support allocative and productive efficiency gains from consolidation of school districts and general-purpose governments, this evidence is not conclusive. The issues of urban poverty, inequitable economic opportunities, residential segregation, and urban sprawl would keep alive the debate over regionalism and localism in urban governance.

Chapter 4

A Theoretical Consideration of How School Choice and Political Institutions Affect Funding Inequity

INTRODUCTION

State constitutions and statutes, with the exception of Hawaii, have delegated major responsibility and political authority for operating and financing public schools to local school districts (Belfield and Levin 2005a; Gordon 2015; Peterson 1981; Springer et al. 2015). In most cases, school districts have the legal/political authority to raise local resources for providing K-12 education within their jurisdictions. However, a significant number of school districts have no legal fiscal authority and must rely on the state or other local governments for funding (Berkman and Plutzer 2005). In most cases, the parent governments of these fiscally dependent school districts raise revenue from property taxes (Picus et al. 2015).

State governments have shouldered increased burden of funding public education mainly to address twin challenges of inequitable provisioning and inequitable outcomes. However, overcoming these challenges seems intractable, though the inequity problem has significantly reduced in magnitude in recent decades (Baker 2018). Since the landmark California Supreme Court decision in *Serrano v. Priest* in 1971 and the famous US Supreme Court's judgment in *Rodriguez v. San Antonio* in 1973, there has been a great deal of activism from judiciary, state, and civil society actors in promoting equity in school districts' spending in the United States. However, in spite of at least a four-decade-long effort at addressing inequity in public education finance, the problem persists (Corcoran and Evans 2015; Evans et al. 1997; Murray et al. 1998), though at a lesser degree than before (Baker 2018). Although state governments' efforts at funding equalization have improved equity in spending, the variation in per-pupil funding across school districts remains

(Berkman and Plutzer 2005; Hertert et al. 1994; Hoxby 1998; Odden and Picus 2013; Wong 1999).

Public school finance is an important topic because it constitutes about 34 percent of total state spending in the United States, which is a lot of money (Baker 2018; US Census of Governments 2007). From a public policy perspective, it is important to clarify which factors explain inequity in school district spending. Important factors include prevailing socioeconomic structure of school districts; various court judgments on equity and adequacy in public education finance; differences in local political institutions; and interest groups. To this end, there are several studies that explain the predictors of inequity in school district spending (Berkman and Plutzer 2005; Berry and Gersen 2009; Corcoran and Evans 2015; Evans et al. 1997; Harris et al. 2001; Murray et al. 1998; Poterba 1997; Wilson et al. 2006). Yet although few studies have examined the effects of interschool district competition (Hoxby 2000; Hoxby 2007; Marlow 2000; Rothstein 2007) on school district spending, none has considered the role of local political institutions. I bring together the theoretical and empirical literature on equity in school district spending, interschool district competition, and political institutions in this chapter. This chapter uses terms such as decentralization and competition interchangeably to convey higher levels of interschool district competition in an MA. Similarly, the use of consolidated school districts conveys lower levels of interschool district competition.

EQUITY IN SPENDING, SCHOOL DISTRICT COMPETITION, AND POLITICAL INSTITUTIONS

In general, levels of per-pupil spending in school districts purportedly ensure equitable provision of public education to all children. Consistent with the fiscal neutrality principle, I study equity in school district spending by examining how local political institutions and interschool district competition explain variation in per-pupil spending by urban school districts that fall in different median household income quintiles within a state. The fiscal neutrality principle implies that local district's wealth should not be a decisive factor in the quality of schooling a child receives, over and above the wealth of the state as a whole (Coons et al. 1970; Ericson 1984; Odden and Picus 2015; Springer et al. 2015). This equality principle does not emphasize equal per-pupil spending across school districts, thereby making room for variation in the cost of providing education. This equity principle also does not require documenting the relationship between education spending and educational outcomes (Koski and Hahnel 2015).

The theoretical literature that examines factors behind levels of local governments spending, in general, and school districts, in particular, falls within five traditions, namely (1) the Public Choice model; (2) the Leviathan model; (3) the Reformism model; (4) the Consolidated Local Governments model; and (5) the Policy Responsiveness model. The major debate in the literature concerns the appropriateness of more decentralized (Ostrom et al. 1961) versus more consolidated forms of local governments (DeHoog et al. 1990; Gordon and Knight 2008; Lowery 2000; Lyons and Lowery 1989) and the role of different types of political institutions (Berkman and Plutzer 2005; Berry and Gersen 2009; Craw 2008) in spending levels and equity.

The Public Choice Model

The basic argument in the Public Choice model is that higher levels of competition between local governments for residents bring economy in local service provision. Local service provision may not be efficient if there are fewer options for residents to realize their choice for most preferred bundle of taxation and local public goods. Proponents of decentralization (or higher levels of interlocal government competition) argue that more local governments in a metropolitan area accommodate heterogeneity in individual preferences for optimal taxes and expenditures on public goods (Ostrom et al. 1961). Pioneered by Tiebout (1956), this argument forms the basis for the Public Choice model. This model is concerned with the choice of efficient levels of goods and services that are made by the residents within a local jurisdiction. In essence, the Public Choice model posits that residential choice of individuals to live in communities with tax–expenditure bundles that match their preferences and budgets brings allocative efficiency (Harris et al. 2001; Hoxby 1994, 1999; Poterba 1997). The basic logic in the Public Choice model is as follows. The communities at the local level seek to attain optimum size[1] for the efficient delivery of public goods and services by local governments. The pursuit of optimum size is essential in order to lower the average cost of public goods and services. The residents reveal their preferences by choosing a package of public goods and services offered by local governments. If the public goods and services are not offered efficiently at some optimum size, the migration of residents will occur until that optimum size has been reached. By choosing to reside in a community with a given package of public goods and services, the residents reveal their preferences or willingness to pay. Consequently, the local government can appropriately tax the community in order to sustain the level of public goods. This simultaneous occurrence of the matching of residents' preferences and attainment of optimum size of the local community ensures both allocative and productive efficiency in the delivery of public goods at the local level (Howell-Moroney 2008; Hoxby 1994, 1999, 2000; Jimenez and Hendrick 2010; Ostrom et al. 1961; Tiebout 1956). The majority of studies on local governments have interpreted these efficiency gains to translate into lower levels of per capita revenue or expenditure (Howell-Moroney 2008; Gordon and Knight 2008; Jimenez and Hendrick 2010; MacDonald 2008).

The Public Choice model is a demand-side perspective in which residents match their preferences with the supply of different tax–expenditure bundles from local governments in a region. Hence, the proponents of public choice argue for the existence of numerous or decentralized local governments in a metropolitan area to capture heterogeneity in citizen demand (Ostrom et al. 1961). Lyons and Lowery (1989, p. 533) note that the decentralized or polycentric model of local government "focuses on the need to maintain numerous units of local governments in each urban area in order to maximize opportunities for individual citizens to choose a tax-service package that best suits their needs."

Subsumed within the Public Choice model is the median voter hypothesis, which provides a practical approach to aggregate citizen preferences for local public goods and services. The median voter hypothesis permits the use of local jurisdiction data for empirical estimation of the Public Choice model (Rubinfield et al. 1987). In particular, income level and tax price of the local median voter drives local government spending on public goods (Ahmed and Greene 2000; Bergstrom and Goodman 1973; Borcherding and Deacon 1972). However, such an estimation suffers from selection bias (also termed as "Tiebout Bias"), because residents may self-select into local communities based on the quantity and quality of public goods provided (Hoxby 2000; Marlow 2000; Millimet and Collier 2008; Millimet and Rangaprasad 2007; Rubinfield et al. 1987). Additionally, a set of common variables may explain matching of residents to communities with their preferred public expenditures and residents' demand for public goods (Rubinfield et al. 1987). This endogeneity problem has further been explained and addressed statistically in the next chapter.

The Leviathan Model

The Leviathan model proposes that the existence of more decentralized and fragmented local governments in a region constrains governments' abilities to impose higher taxation on residents. Such local governments spend less. However, if residents have fewer options for relocation, then they may be taxed at higher rates for a given level of public good. Consequently, local governments spend more. Scholars have argued that greater decentralization of local governments in an MA works against the natural tendency of centralized local governments to extract higher taxes from residents (Brennan and Buchanan 1980; Jimenez and Hendrick 2010). This tendency of governments is also termed "Leviathan behavior" (Brennan and Buchanan

1980; Craw 2008). The Leviathan model explains government size in terms of the magnitude of tax revenue collection and the size of expenditure (Craw 2008; Merrifield 1991, 2000; Nelson 1986; Oates 1985; Poterba 1994, 1996). The central concern of the Leviathan model lies in estimating the relationship between levels of interjurisdictional competition and levels of taxation and spending. This correspondence is termed the monopoly power of local governments (Craw 2000). This central concern also makes it consistent with the Public Choice model as at the practical level of empirically estimating the key propositions of the two theories, the empirical models and measurements are identical.

The Leviathan model is a supply-side view of the organization of local governments in a metropolitan area. Proponents argue that lower levels of interjurisdictional competition in a metropolitan area lead to higher local spending on public goods, because local public officials have the opportunity to raise disproportionately more revenue for satisfying bureaucratic slack and high remuneration (or rent-seeking in Niskanen's terms) as taxpayers have fewer options to relocate to similar jurisdictions in vicinity (Craw 2008; Niskanen 1971; Yeung 2009).

The Consolidated Local Governments Model

Although the Public Choice model takes up a demand-side perspective and the Leviathan model takes up a supply-side perspective, the two models reach the same conclusion that higher levels of interjurisdictional competition within a metropolitan area are associated with lower levels of spending by local governments. In contrast, opponents contend that decentralized local governments cause spillover, such as urban sprawl, and racial and economic segregation. These spillovers bring inefficiency and inequity in local service provision. Consolidated local governments that have jurisdictions over inner-city and suburban regions enjoy economies of scale and can also efficiently and equitably internalize spillovers from interdependent localities. Therefore, they are more efficient and equitable. Howell-Moroney (2008, p. 100) has challenged the central assumptions in the Public Choice model of decentralized local governments vis-a-vis the actual environment in which such polycentric governments work. He cites recent studies (Downs 1994; Dreier et al. 2001; Rusk 1993; Squires 2002) and notes that "the residential segregation of people by race and class and the many costs of sprawl are magnified and augmented by arrangements that defer to multiple local jurisdictions." These spillovers lead to price distortions, and people do not pay true costs associated with a polycentric institutional arrangement. In this way, the preferences of the residents are incorrectly aggregated by the local governments for optimum tax-service package. In regions with higher levels of interjurisdictional competition, the affluent communities in the suburban regions may not be responsive to the demands of potential low-income residents in spite of the latter's willingness to pay within their limited income. For example, low-income citizens have greater demand for social services and affordable housing. But using fiscal zoning and other means as a deterrent, some local governments in the suburbs may not offer social services and affordable housing. Residential mobility of low-income residents is restricted even though they have willingness to reside in such jurisdictions (Howell-Moroney 2008).

Some scholars have therefore argued against the decentralized model of local governments on equity grounds (Lowery 2000; Lyons and Lowery 1989). For example, Lyons and Lowery (1989) argue that any inequity in spending on public goods among the local governments is acceptable on the efficiency criteria under the Public Choice model, because the residents made a conscious decision to live in communities with suitable tax–expenditure offerings. Subsequently, according to Howell-Moroney (2008, p. 98), the problems of sprawl and concentrated poverty are largely due to the existence of municipal boundaries that "circumscribe notions of collective responsibility." Consolidated local governments can overcome these inequalities by internalizing the costs of providing public services (Howell-Moroney 2008). Consequently, decentralized local governments are allocatively and productively inefficient (Altshuler et al. 1999; Burns 1994; DeHoog et al. 1990; Lowery 2000; Lyons and Lowery 1989; Morgan and Morescal 1999; Rusk 1993; Weiher 1991). Proponents argue that more consolidated local governments in a metropolitan area are more equitable and efficient because these local governments enjoy economies of scale and are better able to internalize the external costs associated with urban sprawl and segregation (Gordon and Knight 2008; Howell-Moroney 2008; Jimenez and Hendrick 2010). In contrast to the fragmented local governments, the consolidated local governments provide public goods and services at lower average per unit price (Jimenez and Hendrick 2010).

However, in response to these criticisms, proponents of Public Choice model argue that with suitable policy designs, the effects of fragmented local governments on spending and outcomes are both productively efficient and equitable. For example, in the context of school districts, Hoxby (1996a) argues that greater interschool district competition is productively efficient and distributionally equitable if it is complemented with means-tested vouchers. Godwin and Kemerer (2002) also make similar arguments in regard to the effects of vouchers on educational outcomes. The consolidation of school finance, on the other hand, results in a situation where loss in productive efficiency outweighs any gains in equity (Hoxby 1996a). Public choice scholars also argue that the rent-seeking goals of public officials and interest groups will reduce allocative efficiency and will reduce the likelihood that funding will go to where it is most needed. To the extent that interest groups are active and represent producers and to the extent that politicians attempt to capture some portion of the rents they produce, allocative efficiency will be reduced.

The Reformism Model

The Reformism model is distinct from the previous models because it focuses on how the structure of political institutions influences local government spending. The key argument in the reformism model is that if elected officials of a local government exercise less direct control over budgets then that local government would spend less in comparison to a local government where local elected officials have more direct control over budgets. This direct control over budgets permits elected officials to cater to narrow constituency demands. Under the scenario of limited direct budget control, elected officials adopt residents' preferred level of spending on public education. Whereas the Public Choice and the Consolidated Local Government models do not formally hypothesize the role of local political institutions, the Leviathan model simply uses the logic of the role of bureaucratic slack and high remuneration in explaining higher levels of local government spending. The latter also offers little guidance on the appropriate type of local government for controlling budget maximizing tendencies of the bureaucracy (Craw 2008). Concerned with bureaucratic slack and other inefficiencies, reformists argue that the type of local government also matters in controlling inflated public budgets and inefficiencies in local taxation and spending (Craw 2008; Feiock et al. 2003; Frant 1996).

In particular, reformists argue that the council–manager form of local government and at-large council elections are better than the mayor–council form of local government and ward-based council elections in allocating public services. The elected officials in the mayor–council form of government have more direct control over the local government budget. Elected officials have the incentive to reward their supporters for gaining votes and hence stay in office. For rewarding more constituents, elected officials may inflate local taxes and spending (Craw 2008). The council–manager form of government, on the other hand, relies on bureaucratic expertise and consensual decision-making where the bureaucrats have increased control over the local government budgets and policymaking. The elected officials' lack of direct control over budgets limits their revenue inflating (or rent-seeking) behavior (Craw 2008). However, council members' lack of expertise may constrain their ability to monitor the performance of bureaucrats. This absence of effective monitoring may induce bureaucrats to engage in rent-seeking behavior (Craw 2008; Frant 1996; Frederickson et al. 2004).

The Policy Responsiveness Model

Local political institutions constantly make policy choices differentially from among several and often competing, policy options that match with citizen preferences for desired policy outcomes. However, forms of political institutions that cannot objectively evaluate broader constituency needs (e.g., ward-based v. at-large elected school boards) will poorly translate citizens' demands into policy outcomes. Similar to the reformism model, the Policy Responsiveness model explicitly hypothesizes the role of political institutions in local government spending. However, the two models make different hypotheses regarding the role of political institutions in local government spending. Whereas political institutions moderate the effect of interlocal government competition on local spending in the reformism model, they moderate the effect of citizen demand on local spending and other policy outcomes in the Policy Responsiveness model (Berkman and Plutzer 2005). By policy responsiveness, the authors imply correspondence between public taste for education spending and actual budgetary allocation of the local school district. Berkman and Plutzer (2005) argue that different types of local political institutions play differential roles in translating citizen preferences for desired policy outcomes, because local political institutions constantly make policy choices from among several, and often competing, policy options. For example, at-large elected or appointed school boards are better suited to bring in policy responsiveness in comparison to seemingly more democratic forms of school boards such as districts with ward-based members or districts that allow annual budgets to be passed at annual town hall meetings (Berkman and Plutzer 2005). School districts with at-large school boards objectively assess the broader constituency preferences, while the latter category of local political institutions either cater to narrower constituency preferences or the turnouts in the meetings are not representative of local residents (Berkman and Plutzer 2005).

The Empirical Literature

The empirical literature on local government, in general, and school districts, in particular, offers divergent findings on local government spending and student achievement (see Andrews et al. 2002; Belfield and Levin 2005a; Craw 2008; Gordon and Knight 2008; Hoxby 2000; Howell-Moroney 2008; Rothstein 2007). Since the focus of the public choice, the Leviathan, and the Consolidated Local Government models is on levels of decentralization versus consolidation of local governments in an MA in explaining local government spending, the section below includes the review of empirical studies on the topic.

Public Choice, Consolidated Local Government, and Leviathan Models

Empirical studies on the virtues of decentralized versus consolidated forms of local governments are inconclusive (Howell-Moroney 2008; Jimenez and Hendrick 2010). Some studies have found evidence that higher levels of interjurisdictional competition lead to lower spending (Boyne 1992; Oakerson 1999). Citizens of smaller jurisdictions show greater satisfaction with law enforcement compared to residents of bigger communities (Ostrom 1976; Ostrom et al. 1978; Ostrom and Smith 1976). In contrast, overall citizen satisfaction did not vary systematically between the two governmental structures (DeHoog et al. 1990). Also, decentralization of local governments leads to racial segregation (Altshuler et al. 1999; Burns 1994; Morgan and Morescal 1999; Rusk 1993; Weiher 1991).

The concern regarding urban sprawl has also been empirically evaluated. Analyzing a sample of 822 metropolitan counties, Caruthers (2003) finds that decentralization of municipal and special district governments increased growth outside of incorporated areas. Other studies report similar findings (Carruthers and Ulfarsson 2002; Fulton et al. 2001; Rusk 1993). The empirical literature on the Leviathan model is mixed (Campbell 2004; Craw 2008; Yeung 2009). Eberts and Gronberg (1990) and Zax (1989) support the Leviathan model, while Dolan (1990) and Oates (1985) find no evidence. Campbell (2004) offers mixed findings. Greater interlocal government competition was associated with higher city expenditures and government size (Dolan 1990; Santerre 1991). Higher level of decentralization is associated with lower level of government spending (Lalvani 2002; Rodden 2003; Zax 1989). Clearly, these studies do not offer indisputable evidence in favor of either of the arguments that more competition between local jurisdictions or consolidated local governments spends less and is more equitable. This lack of consensus in the empirical literature warrants further empirical studies with new contexts and new data. Analyses of school district expenditures provide an opportunity to conduct such studies.

The Reformism Model

The empirical evidence that tests the reformism model offers mixed results (Craw 2008). Lyons (1978) and Stumm and Corrigan (1998) present supporting evidence, while Farnham (1990) and Hayes and Chang (1990) find no evidence. For example, Stumm and Corrigan (1998) report that per capita government expenditure is higher in mayor–council cities than in council–manager cities. Examining five public expenditure categories on US city-level data, Saha (2011) reports that the mayor–council form of government spends more than the council–manager form of government for only police and highways. The form of local government, however, did not matter in explaining fire expenditure, sewerage expenditure, and parks and recreational expenditure. Farnham (1990) reported that the council–manager form of local government has no significant effect on public spending. Empirical results in Jung (2006) and MacDonald (2008) confirm Farnham's findings and indicate that the form of local government has no effect on governments' expenditure decisions. It is evident that in the context of municipal and county governments, empirical studies on the reformism model offer contradictory findings. Moreover, there is an absence of a similar empirical study in the context of school districts in the United States. This book fills this gap.

The Policy Responsiveness Model

Utilizing public opinion survey data, Berkman and Plutzer (2005) have studied policy responsiveness in school district spending by estimating the moderating effects of citizen preferences by political institutions. While Berkman and Plutzer (2005) have attempted a complex approach to estimate citizen demand for testing their Policy Responsiveness hypotheses, there are no other studies following a similar approach in the context of public education. Direct estimation of residents' demand for public education through the use of cumulative national representative sample of General Social Survey and the multilevel modeling technique is indeed a major contribution. However, Berkman and Plutzer (2005) have argued in favor of the validity of their measure of public opinion by showing a strong correlation with median housing values. The latter is an indirect measure of residents' demand for public education spending often used by economists (Ahmed and Greene 2000; Rubinfield et al. 1987). This implies that both direct and indirect measures are not substantively different. Also, the use of a national sample for estimating local constituent units is not without problems. Cnudde (2006) notes: "Because of the stratifying and clustering factors in a national sample, the conclusion that a sample—no matter how large—is representative of a component unit smaller than the nation, such as a state, or a congressional or school, is problematic" (2006, p. 588). Moreover, the data on proxy measures of citizen demand, such as median housing values and median income, are readily available for estimating the policy responsiveness of school districts.

Synthesizing the Five Models

In light of the multiplicity of theoretical models and corresponding inconclusive empirical literature on each of them, it is pertinent to bring together consistent elements of the theoretical and empirical literature for understanding equity in local governments' spending. In this regard, Craw (2008) has synthesized the public choice, the Leviathan and the reformism models of public spending at the local level recently and proposed the "Tamed Leviathan Hypothesis" for explaining local government spending. However, Craw (2008) applied the "Tamed Leviathan Hypothesis" to municipal governments spending and not school districts. His general approach, however, is applicable to the study of spending behavior of all types of local governments including school districts. Craw (2008) argues that the Leviathan and the reformism models are not inconsistent, and that a comprehensive model of local public finance would have to incorporate consistent elements of both models. Higher public spending with lower levels of interjurisdictional competition occurs because residents and businesses in such communities do not have a choice to "vote with their feet." These local governments face less competition and have greater economic capacity to inflate public budgets and hence squeeze higher levels of taxation from residents. However, the Leviathan model is silent on the question as to why and how the local governments would extract higher taxes from residents, given the democratic political setup (Craw 2008).

Similarly, studies on the reformism model seek to explain relatively inflated public budgets and higher levels of taxation by the mayor–council form of local government in comparison to the council–manager form because of incentives and opportunities created by different types of political institutions for economic exploitation. However, the literature review suggests that the evidence for this relationship is weak. There is a parallel to this argument while comparing elected officials of ward-based local boards to at-large elected members or elected or appointed school superintendents. This type of behavior of the locally elected officials is simply explained in terms of greater and direct control over the distribution of funds from the local government budget. Craw (2008) argues that the reformism hypothesis does not explicitly explain how local governments assume economic capacity to act in their self-interest. There is an implicit assumption that local governments tend to behave as monopolies under certain types of political institutions.

Craw's Tamed Leviathan Hypothesis has attempted to answer the theoretical shortcomings of the Leviathan and Reformism models by synthesizing and integrating them (Craw 2008). Furthermore, Craw's Tamed Leviathan Hypothesis includes control variables that measure local citizen demand for public services or what Berkman and Plutzer (2005) term as citizen preferences. Craw posits that political institutions moderate the effect of interlocal government competition in an MA on local government spending. In the context of municipal governments, Craw hypothesizes that higher levels of decentralization/fragmentation of local governments lead to lower spending, but this spending depends on the type of political institution. Higher levels of decentralization restrict the capacity of elected officials with more direct control over budgets from spending more than elected officials with less direct control over budgets. With lower levels of centralization, residents have fewer options to relocate to other local jurisdictions, and hence they can be taxed at higher rates for a given level of public good. However, some forms of political institutions can objectively take broader constituency perspectives and spend fewer dollars even when there is less decentralization.

Craw's Tamed Leviathan model seemingly encompasses the Public Choice model (and its byproduct of the median voter hypothesis), the Leviathan model, and the Reformism model. Additionally, Craw's approach is consistent with the Policy Responsiveness theory developed by Berkman and Plutzer (2005). Both Craw (2008) and Berkman and Plutzer (2005) emphasize the important role of local demand and political institutions in provisioning of collective goods. However, there are five notable differences between the two. First, the unit of analysis in Craw (2008) is municipal governments, while the school district is the unit of analysis in Berkman and Plutzer (2005). This difference is minor because school districts and municipalities are both local government institutions. However, intergovernmental revenues from federal and state sources constituted 3.75 percent and 29 percent, respectively, for all local governments in 2007[2] in contrast to 9 percent and 40 percent, respectively, for the school districts. Second, Berkman and Plutzer (2005) have directly estimated the public preferences by deriving public opinion from the national sample of General Social Survey. Craw (2008) has indirectly measured public preferences for public services by including measures for poverty, nonwhite population, population of foreign-born residents, nonwhite council members, population over 65, and homeownership. Craw (2008) treats median housing value as an indicator of the supplying capacity of local governments, whereas Berkman and Plutzer (2005) treat it as an indicator of resident demand. Third, the Policy Responsiveness model does not include a measure of the level of interlocal government competition in an MA, which is one of the central variables of concern in the Tamed Leviathan Hypothesis. This difference would disappear if the Policy Responsiveness model included explanations for differences in local government spending. It would then be possible to include the level of interlocal government competition in an MA as an explanatory factor in local government spending. Such a possibility exists because Berkman and Plutzer (2005, p. 6) recognize the importance of controlling for "the effects of economics and resources" in empirical estimation of the Policy Responsiveness model. Fourth, political institutions interact with public preferences in the Policy Responsiveness model, while in the Tamed Leviathan Hypothesis they interact with the interlocal government competition in an MA. Finally, out of the two measures of interest group strength in the Policy Responsiveness model, the Tamed Leviathan Hypothesis includes the elderly population, but ignores employee unions. The Policy Responsiveness model hypothesizes that interest groups moderate the effects of public opinion on local spending.

THE PROPOSED CONCEPTUAL MODEL

Barring the last two, the other differences between the Tamed Leviathan Hypothesis and the Policy Responsiveness model are not difficult to reconcile. For example, as noted above, a study of spending levels of local governments in urban regions can include measures of interlocal government competition in an MA without contradicting the basic hypotheses of the Policy Responsiveness model. The difference concerning the empirical testing of interactions between political institutions and residents' demands for public services is challenging and cumbersome in the absence of a single measure for residents' demand.

This practical challenge is also applicable to the empirical estimation of hypothesized interactions between measures of interest groups and public opinion (i.e., the measure of resident's demand). There are several reasons for not including the two interactions in an empirical model for estimating equity in local government spending. First, estimation of local public opinion with data on higher levels of political units may be inaccurate (Cnudde 2006); this book instead uses several conventional demographic and economic variables, such as poverty, nonwhite population, population of foreign-born residents, log of district population, nonwhite council members, education levels of the population, and homeownership (Harris et al. 2001; Craw 2008). These variables capture some of the heterogeneity among districts which may explain preferences for school spending (Harris et al. 2001). Interactions of several measures for political institutions and interest groups with each of the demographic and economic variables would be empirically unmanageable and would not be parsimonious. Second, inclusion of some of the important covariates in Berkman and Plutzer (2005), such as interest groups as control variables, maintains the focus of this book on estimating the equity implications of political institutions and interlocal government competition in a MA for school district spending. Third, the direct estimation of public opinion (or resident demand) does not address the "Tiebout Bias" in interlocal government sorting of residents. According to Bayer and Timmins (2007, p. 353), "the central problem in an empirical application is simply that of distinguishing the aggregate behavioral effect of local spillovers from that of fixed natural advantages that are tied to locations, particularly when the latter are not observed by the researcher." As will be explained in the methodology section in the next chapter, this book tackles this empirical problem by utilizing fixed effects and instrumental variable fixed effects panel data models.

This book extends the "Tamed Leviathan Hypothesis" in Craw (2008) by considering the intersection of within-state rankings of school districts' median household income, political institutions, and interschool district competition. I term this model as "Extended Tamed Leviathan Model." This model integrates the Consolidation model in formulating hypotheses in opposite direction to the key arguments in the Tamed Leviathan model above. This is so because the Leviathan and the Consolidation models predict opposing effects of interlocal competition/decentralization on local government spending. The mechanism in the Tamed Leviathan model also applies here, albeit in opposite direction. Consolidation of suburban regions with inner-city provides economies of scale. Such local governments can also efficiently and equitably manage spillovers from interdependent localities. However, some forms of political institutions may cater to narrower constituency needs and hence may spend higher dollars even when there is less decentralization. Table 4.1 summarizes the key argument, sources of inefficiency and mechanisms through which each of the models discussed above affects equity in local government spending and productive efficiency in educational outcomes. Figure 4.1 proposes the conceptual model that synthesizes the models explained in the preceding.

HYPOTHESES

The Extended Tamed Leviathan model provides hypotheses that propose equity effects of political institutions and interschool district competition in an MA on school district spending. Moreover, since the proponents of local government consolidation formulate hypotheses contrary to the public choice and Leviathan models, the empirical estimation of the Extended Tamed Leviathan model presents the necessary evidence to compare and contrast the competing perspectives. This is possible by formulating hypotheses in opposite direction corresponding to each of the relevant hypothesis of the Tamed Leviathan model. The latter corresponds to the interactive effect of interjurisdictional competition and political institutions on equity in school district spending. Therefore, the Extended Leviathan model leads to hypotheses and sub-hypotheses in pairs. For each pair, the first hypothesis/sub-hypothesis is consistent with the Tamed Leviathan model and the second is consistent with the Consolidated Local Governments model. The sub-hypotheses will be noted and explained as expected relationships when I present results of my regression models, but the main hypotheses are as below:

> The Tamed Leviathan Model: Overall, with an increase in inter-school district competition the school districts spend less but political institutions moderate this relationship.

> The Consolidation Model: Overall, with an increase in inter-school district competition the school districts spend more but political institutions moderate this relationship.

Table 4.1 Key Arguments in the Theoretical Models Concerning Efficiency and Equity in Local Government

Models	Key Efficiency / Equity Argument	Policy Outcome / Feature		Discussion of Equity
		Sources of Inefficiency	Mechanism of Inefficiency	
The Public Choice Model	Higher levels of competition between local governments for residents bring efficiency and economy in local service provision. These governments spend less.	Fewer local governments in a region and concentration of residents in fewer of these local governments.	Fewer options for residents to realize their choice for most preferred bundle of taxation and local public goods.	No
The Leviathan Model	The decentralization hypothesis of the Leviathan model implies that the existence of more decentralized/ fragmented local governments in a region constrains them in imposing higher taxation on residents. Such local governments spend less.	Fewer local governments in a region.	Residents have fewer options to relocate to other local jurisdictions, and hence they can be taxed at higher rates for a given level of public good.	No
The Consolidation Model	Higher levels of competition between local governments for residents cause sprawl and segregation. These spillovers bring inefficiency and inequity in local service provision. Consolidated local governments that have jurisdictions over inner-city and suburban regions enjoy economies of scale and can internalize spillovers. Therefore, they are more efficient and equitable. Such local governments spend less.	More local governments in a region lead to flight of affluent residents from inner-city to suburbs. Suburban localities prevent low-income and minority population from residing there.	Consolidation of suburban regions with inner-city regions provides economies of scale. Such local governments can also efficiently and equitably manage spillovers from interdependent localities.	Yes

(Continued)

Table 4.1 Key Arguments in the Theoretical Models Concerning Efficiency and Equity in Local Government (*Continued*)

Models	Policy Outcome / Feature			
	Key Efficiency / Equity Argument	*Sources of Inefficiency*	*Mechanism of Inefficiency*	*Discussion of Equity*
The Reformism Model	If elected officials of a local government exercise less direct control over budgets, then that local government would spend less in comparison to a local government where local elected officials have more direct control over budgets.	Type of local governing political institution and direct control over budgets.	The political institutions that have the incentive to cater to narrow constituency demands will ignore the preferred level of spending on public education by the residents and hence spend more.	No
The Policy Responsiveness Model	Different types of local political institutions constantly make policy choices differentially from among several, and often competing policy options that match with citizen preferences for desired policy outcomes.	More democratic forms of school boards (e.g., ward-based v. at-large elected school boards) and miscalculation of local needs.	The forms of political institutions that cannot objectively evaluate broader constituency needs (e.g., ward-based v. at-large elected school boards) will poorly translate citizens' demand into policy outcomes.	No
The Tamed Leviathan Model	Higher levels of decentralization/ fragmentation of local governments lead to lower spending, but this spending depends on the type of political institution. Higher level of decentralization restricts the capacity of elected officials with more direct control over budgets from spending more than elected officials with less direct control over budgets.	Fewer local governments in a region, the type of local political institution and direct control over budgets.	Residents have fewer options to relocate to other local jurisdictions and hence they can be taxed at higher rates for a given level of public good. However, some forms of political institutions can objectively take broader constituency perspective and spend lower dollars even when there is less decentralization.	No

| The Extended Tamed Leviathan Model (ETL) | The ETL integrates the Consolidation model in formulating hypotheses in opposite direction to the key arguments in the Tamed Leviathan model. This is so because the Leviathan and the Consolidation models predict opposing effects of interlocal competition/decentralization on local government spending. | Levels of competition between local governments and the type of local political institution | The mechanism in the Tamed Leviathan model also applies here. Consolidation of suburban regions with inner-city provides economies of scale. Such local governments can also efficiently and equitably manage spillovers from interdependent localities. However, some forms of political institutions may cater to narrower constituency needs and hence may spend higher dollars even when there is less decentralization. | Yes |

Source: Author's compilation.

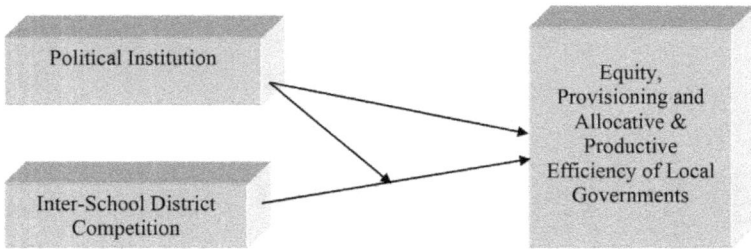

Figure 4.1   The Extended Tamed Leviathan Model. *Source*: Author's own compilation.

For estimating equity implications of interschool district competition and political institutions, two hypotheses are proposed. These hypotheses are consistent with the Consolidated Local Governments model and the Reformism model. First, it is expected that the negative effect of interschool district competition on per-pupil spending of school districts will be more negative for low-income school districts than high-income school districts. Second, it is expected that the relative negative effects of types of political institutions on per-pupil spending of school districts will be more negative for low-income school districts than high-income school districts.

NOTES

1. Size here refers to "the fixed resource of land and the demand conditions of current residents" for public goods in a local political jurisdiction (Dowding et al. 1994, p. 767).

2. Please see the US Census Bureau, State and Local Government Finance at: http://www.census.gov/govs/local/historical_data_2007.html#state_local.

Chapter 5

Empirical Examination of How School Choice and Political Institution Affect Funding Inequity

DATA

For measuring different fiscal variables including this book's dependent variable—the log of per-pupil total expenditure by school districts for fiscal years 1990–1995—the Longitudinal Unified School District Fiscal-Nonfiscal Detail Datafile (UFNFD) that spans fiscal years 1990 to 2002 has been utilized. This data was released by the National Center for Education Statistics (NCES) in 2006 by condensing the Fiscal-Nonfiscal Detail Datafile (FNFD). The NCES provides longitudinal FNFD & UFNFD data for researchers interested in studying changes in the school district-level fiscal or nonfiscal variables over time. The FNFD data for the 15,144 regular school districts has been generated by combining the Local Education Agency (LEA) Universe Survey Longitudinal File for Common Core's nonfiscal data and the school district fiscal (F-33) data for the school years 1989–1990 through 1999–2002 (fiscal years 1990 to 2002). These regular districts serve the vast majority of the nation's public school students (Williams et al. 2006). For example, about 90 percent of total enrolled students were in public schools in the United States in 2009 (U.S. Dept. of Education, National Center of Education Statistics 2012). The UFNFD file combines data from separate but interdependent elementary districts (typically grades K-12) and the secondary districts (typically grades nine to twelve). These two types of school districts constitute "regular districts" in the FNFD file. This natural combination results in records that contain data for each of the unified K-12 "pseudo-district." Therefore, the unified K-12 "pseudo-district" is the one where a secondary school district has captive students from an elementary school district. The folding of the elementary districts (present in the primary longitudinal Fiscal-Nonfiscal Detail file [FNFD]) for regular school districts, (see Williams et al.

2006 for details) into the K-12 pseudo-districts (in the UFNFD) neither lost nor created any students or dollars. Therefore, the UFNFD file has the same aggregate numbers of students and various dollar amounts each year (Williams et al. 2006). The UFNFD[1] file contains one record for each of 11,518 unified and pseudo-unified K-12 districts. This book's sample includes only those K-12 pseudo-unified districts that were geographically located in any of the Metropolitan Areas as defined in the UFNFD data (Williams et al. 2006). For measuring the interschool district competition substantively, other studies have selected sample school districts similarly (Hoxby 2000; Rothstein 2007). Selection of urban school districts in this manner resulted in a panel of 5,017 K-12 pseudo-unified districts for fiscal years 1990 to 1995.[2] Based on the Common Core of Data, these urban pseudo-unified districts enrolled 74.1 percent of nation's public school students in 1990 which rose to 77.5 percent in 1995. The UFNFD data is the source for per-pupil spending, local per-pupil revenue, total per-pupil revenue, total per-pupil revenue from state, student enrollment, region, and FIPS codes for metropolitan area, counties, and states. Since the UFNFD data does not include information on local revenues from property tax sources, the relevant information on the variable from the Common Core of Data, School District Finance Survey (F-33) for each of the sample years have been utilized. Measures for local political institutions have been derived from the Popularly Elected Officials Surveys for years 1987 and 1992 by the Census of Governments of the US Census Bureau. This survey has since been discontinued, and therefore similar analysis on a national scale for more recent time periods is ruled out. Due to this data limitation, the study period is confined to fiscal years between 1990 and 1995. The Census data for school districts from School District Demographics System of the NCES are utilized for demographic and economic variables including school district population, poverty, median household income, homeownership, and median housing value. The Census data for years 1990 and 2000 have been linearly interpolated to derive data for years between 1991 and 1995 (Millimet and Collier 2008; Millimet and Rangaprasad 2007). Following Hirsch and Schumacher (2004), the data on unionization of public sector employees in states was compiled from Hirsch and Macpherson (2003) as a proxy for teachers' unionization. The data on court rulings against state funding system came from Corcoran and Evans (2008).

The ten-year lagged interschool district competition measures have been calculated from the Common Core of Data, School District Finance Survey (F-33) for years 1980, 1981, and 1982 (U.S. Dept. of Education, National Center of Education Statistics 1999). These measures are used as instrumental variables for interschool district competition measures. These instruments are appropriate since some of the extensions of the fixed-effects model, such as Hausman–Taylor and Arellano–Bond models, use lags of the endogenous variables as their instruments (Cameron and Trivedi 2009). Since the codes and boundaries for the metropolitan areas were changed in 1983 and 1993, the matching of metropolitan area level measures for interschool district competition for the ten-year lagged behind with those for the years 1990 to 1995 was not straightforward. The county FIPS have been used to the extent possible to match the lagged competition measures with those for the study years for those metropolitan areas whose codes changed.

MEASUREMENT OF INTERJURISDICTIONAL COMPETITION AND LOCAL POLITICAL INSTITUTIONS

Following the standard practice in the literature, the dependent variable in this chapter is the log of per-pupil total expenditure by school districts (Harris et al. 2001; Hoxby 2000; Craw 2008). Political institutions are measured in three ways following Berkman and Plutzer (2005) and Craw (2008). The first measure indicates whether a school district is fiscally dependent on other local governments. The second political institution measure indicates whether a school district has an elected superintendent. The third variable measures whether the school district's governing board is comprised of all appointed members, all elected at-large members, all ward-based elected members or some members elected at large while others ward-based elected. For maintaining logical time sequence between independent and dependent variables, the data on political institutions for years 1987 and 1992 have been used with the log of per-pupil total expenditure for years 1990 to 1992 and for years 1993 to 1995, respectively.

Consistent with Craw (2008) and others (Belfield and Levin 2005b; Hoxby 2000; Marlow 1997; Rothstein 2007), interschool district competition is measured with two variables. The first measure is one minus the Herfindahl Index of student enrollment shares of school districts and is bounded between 0 and 1. The second measure is the number of school districts per 1,000 students in an MA. A higher value on these MA-level measures indicates a higher level of interschool district competition. The ten-year lagged instruments for interschool district competition are measured similarly.

Following Harris et al. (2001), I define equity as the distribution of school district spending across school districts based on within-state groupings of school districts' median household incomes. Equity is operationalized in terms of regional equity/inequity in school district spending, assessing whether spending varies based on within-state groupings of school districts' median household incomes. School districts are grouped into quintiles according to their within-state median household income rankings.

The empirical literature has relied on several control variables to measure heterogeneity in residents' demand for public education (Berkman and Plutzer 2005; Craw 2008; Harris et al. 2001; Hoxby 2000; MacDonald 2008; Poterba 1997). These variables include the log of the school district population, the log of the MA population, the proportion of school-age population (five to seventeen years), percent of twenty-five years and above population with at least high school diploma, percent of foreign-born population, percent of nonwhite population, racial diversity index in an MA, log of median household income, poverty, percent owner-occupied housing units, median housing value, percent of total revenue from local sources, percent of local revenue from property taxes, log of per-pupil revenue from state sources, percent of 65 years and above population, percent of public sector employees covered under collective bargaining agreements (Hoxby 1996b), percent of nonwhites in school district board, and year dummies. The pooled cross-section models additionally control for state dummies, region and state court rulings against state education funding system. Figure 5.1 presents yearly means and standard deviations for the variables in this chapter.

METHODOLOGY: ESTIMATION STRATEGY

Given the panel nature of the data, the estimation strategy follows that of Harris et al. (2001) and MacDonald (2008). Similar to these studies, variables vary across districts and over time. Each observation on the dependent and independent variables represents district i in state j at time t. For deriving equity implications, the within-state median household income rankings of the school districts have been interacted with local political institutions and interlocal government competition. Harris et al. (2001) used a similar strategy in evaluating the equity implications of court rulings on state fiscal system on public education. Future studies may include other strategies in evaluating equity in school district spending, such as school district rankings on percent of minorities or percent of students with English as their second language.

Pooled OLS models are utilized as the base for both additive and interactive models. For drawing substantive conclusions, however, the results from the fixed-effects and instrumental variable fixed-effects regressions for both additive and interactive models are used. Additionally, postestimation marginal analyses of the results from the fixed-effects and instrumental variable fixed-effects regressions for interactive models are performed to test hypotheses. The following fixed-effects interactive model has been estimated in this book.

The general fixed-effect panel data model takes the following form (Cameron and Trivedi 2009): $Y_{ijt} = \alpha_{ij} + X'_{ijt} \beta + \varepsilon_{ijt}$; where Y_{ijt} is the

Variables / Years	Mean						Std. Dev.					
	990	1991	1992	1993	1994	1995	1990	1991	1992	1993	1994	1995
Per Pupil Total Expenditure	5314.244	5607.904	5742.480	6022.332	6221.938	6452.584	1554.057	1670.829	1692.010	1751.245	1790.705	1823.180
Herfindahl Index of School District Competition	3.762	0.762	0.762	0.762	0.763	0.764	0.237	0.238	0.239	0.240	0.240	0.240
Number of School District Per 1000 Students in Metro Areas	3.159	0.155	0.152	0.149	0.146	0.144	0.126	0.124	0.122	0.120	0.119	0.117
10 Year Lag: Herfindahl Index of School District Competition	3.760	0.761	0.758	0.758	0.757	0.757	0.236	0.237	0.238	0.238	0.239	0.240
10 Year Lag: Number of School District Per 1000 Students in Metro Areas	0.191	0.200	0.207	0.205	0.205	0.204	0.150	0.157	0.169	0.168	0.167	0.167
Appointed School Board	0.113	0.112	0.112	0.098	0.098	0.098	0.317	0.316	0.315	0.298	0.298	0.297
Elected at-Large School Board	0.700	0.702	0.703	0.550	0.551	0.552	0.458	0.458	0.457	0.498	0.497	0.497
Ward-Based Elected School Board	0.120	0.120	0.119	0.253	0.253	0.252	0.325	0.325	0.324	0.435	0.435	0.434
Mixed School Board	0.067	0.066	0.066	0.099	0.098	0.098	0.250	0.248	0.248	0.298	0.297	0.297
Elected School Superintendent	0.072	0.074	0.075	0.032	0.033	0.033	0.259	0.262	0.263	0.177	0.178	0.179
Fiscally Dependent School District	0.180	0.179	0.178	0.178	0.179	0.179	0.384	0.383	0.383	0.383	0.383	0.383
School District Population	531879	540632	545621	550278	555685	559809	1383380	1396183	1405916	1416783	1428407	1438086
Metropolitan Area Population	2293146	2212752	2239840	2264007	2291228	2317606	2483891	2492284	2510792	2526836	2543717	2559111
Percent School Age (5-17 Years) Children	0.181	0.183	0.184	0.185	0.186	0.187	0.031	0.030	0.029	0.029	0.028	0.028
Percent 25 Years Plus: High School and Above Educated	76.391	76.827	77.290	77.744	78.201	78.663	10.043	9.971	9.900	9.832	9.782	9.747
Percent Foreign Born Population	8.917	9.331	9.711	10.029	10.362	10.708	10.042	10.241	10.415	10.549	10.705	10.880
Percent Non-White Population	21.073	21.724	22.372	22.999	23.596	24.132	18.942	18.866	18.943	19.045	19.155	19.267
Racial Diversity Index	0.336	0.346	0.355	0.364	0.372	0.379	0.146	0.149	0.149	0.149	0.150	0.150
Median Household Income	33009.050	34337.620	35681.110	37012.270	38370.820	39764.670	10370.780	10744.230	11136.450	11549.600	11992.370	12467.070
Percent Owner Occupied Housing	63.525	63.686	63.846	64.042	64.242	64.471	14.683	14.658	14.643	14.630	14.635	14.645
Median House Value	105225.100	108456.400	111867.500	115028.100	118296.600	121709.800	66753.030	66523.970	66853.110	67314.570	68089.570	69215.570
Percent Local Revenue from Property Taxes	61.613	61.696	64.351	64.341	64.304	63.365	32.003	31.938	32.506	32.506	32.555	32.616
Percent of Population in Poverty	13.735	13.566	13.378	13.192	12.992	12.788	10.714	10.143	9.607	9.097	8.624	8.217
Percent State Public Sector Employees Under Collective Bargaining Agreements	44.532	44.882	44.839	45.343	46.495	45.534	17.903	18.161	17.609	17.154	17.776	18.472
Percent 65 Years-Plus Population	11.523	11.530	11.542	11.552	11.564	11.576	4.192	4.151	4.106	4.068	4.038	4.018
Court Rulings Against State Funding System	0.320	0.323	0.326	0.325	0.325	0.324	0.467	0.468	0.469	0.469	0.468	0.468
Fiscal Capacity: Percent Per Pupil Revenue from Local Sources	47.928	47.751	47.232	46.694	47.697	46.861	20.221	20.499	20.895	19.883	19.195	18.732
Per Pupil State Revenue	2312.525	2432.322	2511.227	2706.312	2701.525	2874.236	968.448	1041.725	1092.515	1087.688	1087.373	1160.475
Percent Non-White in Governing Board	19.623	19.545	19.471	27.466	27.372	27.244	28.972	28.875	28.841	33.891	33.891	33.871

Figure 5.1 Descriptive Statistics: Year-wise Means and Standard Deviations of the Study Variables. *Source*: Author's own calculations and tabulation.

dependent variable for observation i in region j in time t. X'ijt similarly is the vector of independent variables (regressors). α_{ij} includes random observation, region, and observation within region-specific effects, and ε_{ijt} is an idiosyncratic error. The fixed-effect panel data model handles limited form of endogeneity as it accounts for correlation between α_{ij} and X'ijt. Furthermore, α_{ij} includes such observation-specific information as geographical proximity when the observations are spatial units. Therefore, fixed-effects model addresses the concerns raised in spatial statistical methods in Slagle (2010).

In the context of this study's empirical modeling strategy, the fixed-effects model assumes the following specific form:

log (total per-pupil expenditureijt) = $\beta_1 \times$ interschool district competitionijt + $\beta_2 \times$ political institutionsijt + $\beta_3 \times$ (interschool district competitionijt $\times$ political institutionsijt) + $\beta_4 \times$ (interschool district competitionijt $\times$ median household income quintileijt) + $\beta_5 \times$ (political institutionsijt $\times$ median household income quintileijt) + π Xijt + δ_{ij} + Sjt + ε_{ijt}; where π is the vector of coefficients for control variables Xijt including the intercept and time dummies; δij are district fixed effects that capture those factors that vary across districts but do not change over time, for example, the proximity of one district with the other; Sjt is the state effects to capture the effects of public sector employees covered under collective bargaining agreements; and εijt is the error term.

ADDRESSING ADDITIONAL ENDOGENEITY PROBLEM

The instrumental variable fixed-effects models utilize ten-year lags for the interschool district competition measures in the fixed-effects model described above. The panel data instrumental variable fixed-effects model appropriately transforms the corresponding fixed-effects model to control for district fixed-effects and then applies instrumental variable estimation procedure to the transformed model (Cameron and Trivedi 2009, p. 282). While estimating the effect of interschool district competition, there are two key methodological problems (Belfield and Levin 2005b). First, competition measures are multi-dimensional and difficult to measure simultaneously. This challenge has been addressed in the context of interschool district competition in public education by including two measures. Second, there is identification problem. The level of competition may be endogenous (Belfield and Levin 2005b; Bettinger 2005; Harris et al. 2001; Hoxby 2000; Rothstein 2007). This means that some unobservable factors are part of the random error term and they may be related to both the dependent variable and one or more independent variable (s).

In case of interschool district competition in an MA, some unobservable factors may influence both supply of per-pupil spending and demand for school districts. For example, according to Hoxby (2000) and Slagle (2010), there may be a situation where one district has a highly productive administration for some peculiar reason. This may result in lower funding levels for the district. Additionally, some of the adjoining school districts might want to consolidate with the district to secure gains for their students from the expertise of highly productive administration. But this implies that the number of school districts in the education market would decline thereby reducing the degree of observed choice. In this situation, the unobservable productive administration is simultaneously correlated with the dependent and independent variables. This results in unpredictable bias in the coefficient of the independent variable (Hoxby 2000). The cross-section data requires the use of appropriate instrumental variable (IV) and the two-stage least squares (2SLS) estimation approach (Hoxby 2000; Rothstein 2007). The selected IV should be highly correlated with the endogenous independent variable, but not with the random error in the regression equation (Gujarati 1995; Wooldridge

2006). But finding such an exogenous IV is not an easy task (Gujarati 1995). In the context of panel data used for this chapter, the employed fixed-effects models effectively address the issue of endogeneity which arises from omission of unit-level unmeasured and unobserved time-invariant variables, which may be correlated with both the dependent and independent variables (Cameron and Trivedi 2009; MacDonald 2008). This unit-level information includes spatial proximity to other school districts within the MA and therefore pertinent suggestions in Slagle (2010) are effectively addressed by the fixed-effects model itself. Additionally, however, there may still remain some time-variant omitted variables that may potentially cause endogeneity, and hence the estimated coefficients of the key independent variables may still be biased.[3] This problem is addressed through the use of the instrumental variable fixed-effects model (Cameron and Trivedi 2009; Harris et al. 2001). Following Harris et al. (2001), one measure each for the two interschool district competition variables have been considered that can arguably serve as valid instruments. Harris et al. (2001) instrumented the share of sixty-five-year-plus population in their study period with the ten-year lagged share of fifty-four to sixty-four years population. This book similarly uses the ten-year lagged interschool district competition measures as instruments corresponding to the two interschool district competition measures.

Studies also argue that the endogeneity problem may bias the effect of political institutions on fiscal outcomes of local governments (Berry and Gergen 2009; Persson and Tabellini 2003). However, Berry and Gersen (2009, p. 482) argue that concerns about the endogeneity of political institutions "should be allayed by the fact that electoral institutions are enshrined in longstanding provisions of state constitutions and city charters." The authors therefore suggest that at least in the short run the political institutions should be considered exogenous. Berry and Gersen's arguments apply to this study because political institutions are measured at two points in time that are apart by only five years, a very short time period to change local political institutions through making commensurate changes in the applicable provisions of the state constitutions and city charters.

RESULTS

The descriptive statistics and the results for the pooled OLS, fixed-effects and instrumental variable fixed-effects models are presented in figure 5.1. The table provides descriptive statistics for the variables that are included in different regression models. Table 5.1 presents the main results for models that include types of electoral composition of school district boards as the measure for local political institutions, respectively. Tables 5.2 and 5.3 present

Table 5.1 Effects of Interschool District Competition and Political Institutions (Type of School District Board) on Log of Per-Pupil Spending by School Districts

Variables	Models without Interactions						Models with Interactions			
	Pooled OLS		Fixed Effects		Fixed Effects: IV		Pooled OLS		Fixed Effects	
	Herfindahl index	Enrollment-Weighted Count	Herfindahl Index	Enrollment-Weighted Count	Herfindahl Index	Enrollment-Weighted Count	Herfindahl Index	Enrollment-Weighted Count	Herfindahl Index	Enrollment-Weighted Count
School District Competition	0.040 (0.033)	−0.036 (0.052)	0.806** (0.288)	−0.594 (0.340)	2.100 (4.050)	−1.170 (77.800)	0.312*** (0.069)	0.589*** (0.140)	0.816** (0.284)	−0.829* (0.389)
At-Large District Board	0.080*** (0.016)	0.082*** (0.017)	−0.001 (0.029)	−0.001 (0.030)	0.026 (0.027)	0.038 (0.333)	0.324*** (0.060)	0.170*** (0.020)	0.039 (0.038)	−0.027 (0.054)
Ward-based District Board	0.074*** (0.020)	0.076*** (0.020)	−0.012 (0.028)	−0.012 (0.029)	0.031 (0.027)	0.043 (0.325)	0.299*** (0.064)	0.152*** (0.028)	0.041 (0.037)	−0.073 (0.054)
Mixed District Board	0.094*** (0.019)	0.096*** (0.020)	0.000 (0.030)	0.003 (0.032)	0.029 (0.028)	0.040 (0.411)	0.292*** (0.063)	0.175*** (0.035)	0.059 (0.046)	−0.029 (0.058)
At-Large DB *Competition							−0.311*** (0.067)	−0.708*** (0.138)		0.395 (0.214)
Ward DB *Competition							−0.275*** (0.071)	−0.625*** (0.152)		0.608** (0.220)
Mixed DB *Competition							−0.235** (0.072)	−0.570*** (0.152)		0.527* (0.217)
2nd Qntl							−0.050 (0.046)	−0.115** (0.040)	0.061 (0.033)	0.066* (0.029)
3rd Qntl							0.049 (0.039)	−0.050 (0.027)	0.107* (0.045)	0.105* (0.047)
4th Qntl							0.024 (0.046)	−0.058 (0.030)	0.099* (0.040)	0.086* (0.041)
Top Qntl							−0.006 (0.056)	−0.006 (0.045)	0.018 (0.040)	−0.007 (0.042)
2nd Qntl *Competition							−0.019 (0.044)			
3rd Qntl*Competition							−0.113** (0.040)			
4th Qntl *Competition							−0.090* (0.044)			
Top Qntl *Competition							−0.018 (0.052)			
2nd Qntl *At-Large DB							0.007 (0.031)	0.053 (0.038)	−0.045 (0.033)	−0.051 (0.029)

	(1)	(2)	(3)	(4)	(5)	(6)	(7)	(8)	(9)	(10)
3rd Qntl *At-Large DB							-0.052*	-0.049*	-0.109*	-0.109*
							(0.024)	(0.022)	(0.046)	(0.049)
4th Qntl *At-Large DB							-0.044	-0.043	-0.112**	-0.102*
							(0.026)	(0.026)	(0.042)	(0.044)
Top Qntl *At-Large DB							-0.052	-0.078*	-0.015	0.004
							(0.031)	(0.035)	(0.040)	(0.044)
2nd Qntl *Ward DB							0.019	0.071	-0.074*	-0.068*
							(0.035)	(0.043)	(0.034)	(0.031)
3rd Qntl *Ward DB							-0.073**	-0.064*	-0.117*	-0.109*
							(0.024)	(0.025)	(0.049)	(0.050)
4th Qntl *Ward DB							-0.046	-0.037	-0.125**	-0.101*
							(0.026)	(0.029)	(0.043)	(0.044)
Top Qntl *Ward DB							-0.059	-0.073	-0.029	0.010
							(0.034)	(0.037)	(0.038)	(0.043)
2nd Qntl *Mixed DB							-0.006	0.033	-0.057	-0.062
							(0.045)	(0.011)	(0.017)	(0.044)
3rd Qntl *Mixed DB							-0.048	-0.041	-0.123*	-0.114
							(0.036)	(0.039)	(0.061)	(0.063)
4th Qntl *Mixed DB							-0.064	-0.060	-0.121*	-0.102
							(0.040)	(0.039)	(0.052)	(0.054)
Top Qntl *Mixed DB							-0.094*	-0.118**	-0.091	-0.062
							(0.043)	(0.044)	(0.056)	(0.058)
Intercept	6.080***	6.040***	5.320**	6.240***	2.550	5.040	5.300***	5.430***	5.340**	6.160***
	(0.438)	(0.453)	(1.670)	(1.660)	(3.240)	(52.100)	(0.467)	(0.477)	(1.630)	(1.570)
R^2 (Within for FE Models)			0.467	0.467	0.415	0.416			0.470	0.472
R^2 (Between)			0.240	0.237	0.173	0.210			0.240	0.260
R^2 (Overall)			0.251	0.254	0.177	0.226			0.250	0.276
Correlation: time-invariant school district effects and Xb	0.771	0.771	-0.526	-0.427	-0.768	-0.515	0.786	0.784	-0.522	-0.373
First-stage F-statistics					182.67***	923.95***				
N	25419	25419	25494	25494	23821	23803	25419	25419	25494	25494

Source: Author's own calculations and tabulation.

[a] ***=p<0.001; **=p<0.01; *=p<0.05.

[b] All the models include log of school district population, Proportion of school-age population (5–17 years), Percent of >25 years population with at least high school diploma, Percent of foreign born population, Percent of nonwhite population, Racial Diversity Index in MSA, Log of median household income, Poverty, Percent of owner-occupied housing units, Median housing value, Percent of total revenue from local sources, Percent of local revenue from property taxes, Log of per-pupil revenue from state sources, Percent of >65 years population, Percent of public sector employees covered under collective bargaining agreements, Percent of nonwhites in School District Board, and Year dummies.

[c] The pooled cross-section models additionally control for State dummies, Region, and State court rulings against education funding system.

[d] Numbers in brackets are standard errors.

Table 5.2   Effects of Interschool District Competition and Political Institutions (Elected School Superintendent) on Log of Per-Pupil Spending by School Districts

| | Models without Interactions | | | | | | Models with Interactions | | | | |
| | Pooled OLS | | Fixed Effects | | Fixed Effects: IV | | Pooled OLS | | Fixed Effects | | Fixed Effects: IV |
Variables	Herfindahl Index	Enrollment-Weighted Count	Herfindahl Index	Enrollment-Weighted Count	Herfindahl Index	Enrollment-Weighted Count	Herfindahl Index	Enrollment-Weighted Count	Herfindahl Index	Enrollment-Weighted Count	Herfindahl Index
School Dist Competition	0.047	−0.021	0.748**	−0.375	2.090	−0.021	0.089	−0.047	0.763**	−0.386	2.060
	(0.033)	(0.054)	(0.281)	(0.339)	(3.850)	(380.000)	(0.047)	(0.054)	(0.284)	(0.339)	(3.160)
Elected Superintendent	0.028	0.028	0.071**	0.070**	0.060***	0.061	0.038	−0.050	−0.018	−0.015	−0.022
	(0.019)	(0.019)	(0.022)	(0.022)	(0.016)	(1.550)	(0.032)	(0.029)	(0.010)	(0.010)	(0.022)
El_Supdt *Competition							−0.081*				
							(0.038)				
2nd Qntl							−0.100*	−0.075***	0.015	0.016	0.002
							(0.049)	(0.016)	(0.025)	(0.024)	(0.010)
3rd Qntl							0.022	−0.102***	0.006	0.006	−0.010
							(0.038)	(0.018)	(0.027)	(0.027)	(0.018)
4th Qntl							0.004	−0.102***	−0.009	−0.009	−0.019
							(0.045)	(0.022)	(0.031)	(0.031)	(0.021)
Top Qntl							−0.014	−0.077**	−0.006	−0.008	−0.022
							(0.059)	(0.028)	(0.033)	(0.032)	(0.024)
2nd Qntl *Competition							0.042				
							(0.058)				
3rd Qntl *Competition							−0.153***				
							(0.046)				
4th Qntl *Competition							−0.127*				
							(0.055)				

	(1)	(2)	(3)	(4)	(5)	(6)	(7)	(8)	(9)	(10)	(11)
Top Qntl *Competition							−0.080 (0.072)				
2nd Qntl *EI_Supdt							0.090** (0.035)	0.077** (0.025)	0.074* (0.029)	0.072** (0.028)	0.120 (0.098)
3rd Qntl *EI_Supdt							0.023 (0.028)	0.085** (0.026)	0.071*** (0.019)	0.069*** (0.019)	0.078* (0.033)
4th Qntl *EI_Supdt							0.054 (0.036)	0.104** (0.033)	0.100** (0.033)	0.095** (0.033)	0.098*** (0.031)
Top Qntl *EI_Supdt							0.014 (0.036)	0.048 (0.031)	0.106*** (0.028)	0.104*** (0.028)	0.100*** (0.029)
Intercept	6.320*** (0.449)	6.260** (0.462)	5.590*** (1.610)	6.340*** (1.610)	2.610 (3.010)	4.340 (3.290)	5.740*** (0.501)	5.770*** (0.510)	5.550*** (1.630)	6.310*** (1.630)	2.460 (2.560)
R² (Within, FE Models)			0.471	0.471	0.415	0.419			0.472	0.471	0.416
R² (Between)			0.233	0.245	0.172	0.304			0.231	0.242	0.175
R² (Overall)	0.769	0.768	0.246	0.264	0.177	0.315	0.779	0.776	0.244	0.261	0.180
Correlation: time-invariant school district effects and Xb			−0.486	−0.353	−0.766	−0.327			−0.496	−0.363	−0.761
First-stage F-statistics					196.03***	1002.09***					148.14***
N	25419	25419	25494	25494	23821	23803	25419	25419	25494	25494	23821

Source: Author's own calculations and tabulation.

[a] ***=p<0.001; **=p<0.01; *=p<0.05.

[b] All the models include log of school district population, log of MSA population, Proportion of school-age population (5–17 years), Percent of >25 years population with at least high school diploma, Percent of foreign born population, Percent of nonwhite population, Racial Diversity Index in MSA, Log of median household income, Poverty, Percent of owner-occupied housing units, Median housing value, Percent of total revenue from local sources, Percent of local revenue from property taxes, Log of per-pupil revenue from state sources, Percent of >65 years population, Percent of public sector employees covered under collective bargaining agreements, Percent of nonwhites in School District Board, and Year dummies.

[c] The pooled cross-section models additionally control for State dummies, Region, and State court rulings against education funding system.

[d] Numbers in brackets are standard errors.

Table 5.3 Effects of Interschool District Competition and Political Institutions (Dependent School Districts) on Log of Per-Pupil Spending by School Districts

Variables	Models without Interactions				Models with Interactions			
	Pooled OLS		Random Effects		Pooled OLS		Random Effects	
	Herfindahl Index	Enrollment-Weighted Count	Herfindahl Index	Enrollment-Weighted Count	Herfindahl Index	Enrollment-Weighted Count	Herfindahl Index	Enrollment-Weighted Count
School Dist Competition	0.029	−0.053	−0.158	0.031	−0.007	−0.112*		0.053
	(0.032)	(0.052)	(0.086)	(0.085)	(0.051)	(0.050)		(0.085)
Dependent School Districts	−0.157***	−0.163***	−0.140***	−0.140***	−0.357***	−0.348***		−0.043
	(0.042)	(0.042)	(0.034)	(0.035)	(0.059)	(0.046)		(0.085)
Dep Sch dist*Competition					0.254***	0.992***		−0.460*
					(0.057)	(0.159)		(0.192)
2nd Income Quintile					−0.035			
					(0.040)			
3rd Income Quintile					−0.004			
					(0.036)			
4th Income Quintile					−0.015			
					(0.040)			
Top Income Quintile					−0.048			
					(0.047)			
2nd Qntl*Competition					−0.026			
					(0.050)			
3rd Qntl*Competition					−0.108*			
					(0.045)			
4th Qntl*Competition					−0.086			
					(0.050)			

Top Qntl*Competition							
					−0.014		
					(0.059)		
Intercept	6.290***	6.290***	4.380***	4.440***	5.933***	6.468***	4.382***
	(0.462)	(0.473)	(0.434)	(0.460)	(0.516)	(0.456)	(0.461)
R^2 (Within: RE Models)	0.397	0.397	0.397	0.397	0.397	0.397	0.397
R^2 (Between)			0.631	0.624			0.629
R^2 (Overall)	0.773	0.773	0.594	0.589	0.785	0.778	0.593
N	25419	25419	25494	25494	25419	25419	25494

Source: Author's own calculations and tabulation.

[a] ***=p<0.001; **=p<0.01; *=p<0.05.

[b] All the models include log of school district population, log of MSA population, Proportion of school-age population (5–17 years), Percent of >25 years population with at least high school diploma, Percent of foreign born population, Percent of nonwhite population, Racial Diversity Index in MSA, Log of median household income, Poverty, Percent of owner-occupied housing units, Median housing value, Percent of total revenue from local sources, Percent of local revenue from property taxes, Log of per pupil revenue from state sources, Percent of >65 years population, Percent of public sector employees covered under collective bargaining agreements, Percent of nonwhites in School District Board, and Year dummies.

[c] The pooled cross-section models additionally control for State dummies, Region, and State court rulings against education funding system.

[d] Numbers in brackets are standard errors.

similar results for models including districts with elected or appointed super-intendents and fiscal dependence as the measures for local political institu-tions. These tables present results for only key independent variables and their interaction terms along with aggregate model-specific statistics. The list of the control variables included in each of the models is listed in the notes below each of the three tables. For the main regression results in each of the tables concerning the panel data models (fixed- and random-effects models) with significant interactions, several additional tables present results for mar-ginal analyses to facilitate their substantive interpretations.

The results of the Hausman tests (not shown here) for comparing the fit of fixed-effects models against random-effects models show that the former models are more appropriate for each of the three measures of political institutions. However, for identifying the coefficient for fiscal dependence of school districts (one of the measures for political institutions), a random-effects model is utilized. The fixed-effects model did not identify the said coefficient because the fiscal dependence measure is collinear with time-invariant unobservable factors. When the fixed-effects model is more appropriate than the random-effects model, the results from the latter are biased (Cameron and Trivedi 2009). Therefore, the results in this chapter for fiscal dependence of school districts should be interpreted cautiously and as indicative.

Aggregate Model-Specific Results

Tables 5.1 and 5.2 present regression results from the pooled OLS, fixed effects, and instrumental variable fixed-effects models that include the type of school district board and type of superintendent's office as measures for political institutions. Table 5.3 presents regression results for the pooled OLS and random-effects models that include fiscal dependence of school districts as a measure for political institution. The regression models are weighted by the number of students in school districts.[4] For the fixed-effects models, within mean number of students are used as weight. The instrumen-tal variable fixed-effects models that include the hypothesized interaction terms in table 5.1 are not reported because none of the interactions were significant.

The pooled OLS models in tables 5.1, 5.2, and 5.3 explain about 77–79 percent of the variance in the log of per-pupil total expenditure. The fixed-effects and the instrumental variable fixed-effects models, on the other hand, explain about 18–28 percent of overall variance in the log of per-pupil total expenditure. The random-effects models in table 5.3 explain about 62–63 percent of variance in the log of per-pupil total expenditure. The standard errors reported in the three tables for the pooled OLS, the fixed-effects, and the random-effects models have been adjusted for heteroskedasticity and clustering of school districts within an MA. For the instrumental variable fixed-effects models, tables 5.1 and 5.2 report bootstrap standard errors.

The first-stage results (not shown here) for the additive instrumental variable fixed-effects models in tables 5.1 and 5.2 and interactive instrumental variable fixed-effects model in table 5.2 show that the ten-year lagged Herfindahl index-based measure of interschool district competition is significantly related to the Herfindahl index-based measure of interschool district competition for the study period. The F-statistics (in tables 5.1 and 5.2) on the joint significance of the excluded instrument are 182.67, 196.03, and 148.14 (the associated p-values are less than 0.001) for the instrumental variable fixed-effects models with the type of school district board and the type of superintendent's office as measures for political institutions, respectively. These two results imply that the said instrument is not a weak instrument (Harris et al. 2001; Hoxby 2000).

The first-stage results (not shown here) for the additive instrumental variable fixed-effects models that include the ten-year lagged enrollment-weighted count of school districts in an MA, however, show that the instrument is not significantly related to the enrollment-weighted count of school districts in an MA for the study period. The F-statistics (reported in tables 5.1 and 5.2) on the joint significance of the excluded instruments are 923.95 and 1002.09 (the p-value are less than 0.001). Although the correlation between the ten-year lagged enrollment-weighted count of school districts in an MA and enrollment-weighted count of school districts for the study period is quite high at 0.66, the t-statistics (not shown here) for the variable in question drops substantially. The latter is quite evident because the bootstrap standard errors are magnified by more than 200 times in table 5.1 and more than 1000 times in table 5.2 in comparison to the standard errors for respective fixed-effects models. Together these results suggest that the ten-year lagged enrollment-weighted count of school districts in an MA is a weak instrument for enrollment-weighted count of school districts in an MA for the study period (Cameron and Trivedi 2009, p. 175). However, since the respective coefficients estimated by instrumental variable fixed-effects models for the enrollment-weighted count of school districts in an MA do not substantively differ from that estimated by the corresponding fixed-effects models, it would serve no appreciable purpose to obtain better instruments. Moreover, the corresponding fixed-effects models have partially addressed the endogeneity problem that arises from omitting unobserved time-invariant school district-level factors including factors such as spatial proximity.

Additive Models: Key Results

Results for additive models in tables 5.1, 5.2, and 5.3 show that the inter-school district competition has no effect on the log of total per-pupil expenditure except for the fixed-effects models in tables 5.1 and 5.2 that use Herfindahl index as the measure for interschool district competition. The fixed-effects model in question in table 5.1 shows that raising interschool district competition in an MA from 0 (no competition) to 1 (perfect competition) results in about 81 percent increase in per-pupil total spending by school districts.[5] The corresponding increase for the fixed-effects model that uses the type of superintendent office as a measure for political institution in table 5.2 is 75 percent. However, the corresponding instrumental variable fixed-effects models in tables 5.1 and 5.2 estimate positive coefficients for the Herfindahl index that are not statistically different from zero. Additionally, the additive random-effects model in table 5.3 also reports a coefficient for the Herfindahl index which is statistically not different from zero.

The type of school district board in table 5.1 does not have a significant effect on the log of per-pupil total expenditures in both the fixed effects and instrumental variable fixed-effects models. However, the results from corresponding models in table 5.2 show that school districts with elected superintendents significantly spend about 6–7 percent more per-pupil total dollars than those with appointed superintendents. The results from the corresponding random-effects models in table 5.3 similarly show that fiscally dependent school districts spend about 14 percent less per-pupil total dollars than fiscally independent school districts.

Overall, the additive models offer mixed findings. The two measures for the interschool district competition in an MA have no effect on per-pupil total expenditure by school districts in fixed-effects instrumental variable models. However, the Herfindahl index of interschool district competition has a positive effect in the fixed-effects model (without the instrument). This result is consistent with similar empirical studies. Using instrumental variable regression model on cross-section data, Rothstein (2007) report that interschool district competition has no effect on student achievement. On the other hand, the study by Hoxby (2000) found positive effect of interschool district competition on student achievement and a small but negative effect on per-pupil spending by school districts. Few earlier studies in the context of different type of local governments, such as Dolan (1990) and Forbes and Zampelli (1989) also report similar findings. These results do not robustly support the expected hypotheses pertaining to the public choice, the Leviathan models, and the consolidated local government model. Substantively, these results suggest that interschool district competition does not robustly affect school district spending.

The additive models also offer mixed results in regard to the effects of political institutions on per-pupil spending by school districts. Whereas the type of school board does not influence school district spending, the other two measures of political institutions have significant effects on per-pupil spending by school districts. Using fixed-effects models, a similar study by Mac-Donald (2008) reports no effects of political institutions on log of per-capita total municipal government expenditure. However, consistent with Craw (2008), results in respect of the type of school superintendent's office and the type of fiscal autonomy of school districts support the reformism hypothesis. The reformism hypothesis is supported because accountability to parent local government and efficiency from appointed school superintendent restricts the ability of these school districts in inflating budgets for rent-seeking. The finding in regard to the type of fiscal autonomy of school districts lends support to the hypothesis in the consolidated local governments' model. This implies that the consolidation of school districts with their respective parent local governments results in overall economies of scale (Howell-Moroney 2008), and therefore fiscally dependent school districts spend less than fiscally independent school districts. Overall, the additive models imply that fiscally dependent school districts and those with appointed superintendent spend less.

Interactive Models: Key Results

The interactive models show the joint effects of interschool district competition and local political institutions on school district spending. These models also show the equity effects of interschool district competition and political institutions. Concerning the pooled OLS models with Herfindahl index as the measure for interschool district competition, the interactions between school district competition and political institutions, between school district competition and median household income rankings, and between political institutions and median household income rankings are significant in tables 5.1, 5.2, and 5.3. For the pooled OLS models with student enrollment-weighted count of school districts in an MA, however, the interactions between school district competition and median household income rankings are not significant in tables 5.1, 5.2, and 5.3. Additionally, the interactions between political institutions and median household income rankings are not significant in table 5.3. Among the fixed-effects models with Herfindahl index as the measure for interschool district competition in tables 5.1 and 5.2, only the interactions between political institutions and median household income rankings are significant. Among the fixed-effects models with student enrollment-weighted count of school districts in an MA as the measure for interschool district competition, additionally the interactions between school district competition and political institutions are significant in table 5.1 when the political institution is measured by the type of school district board. The interactive random-effects model with student enrollment-weighted count of school districts in an MA as the measure for interschool district competition in table 5.3 reports that only the interaction between fiscal dependence and interschool district competition is significant.

In regard to the joint effects of interschool district competition and local political institutions on school district spending, tables 5.4 and 5.5 present results for marginal analyses of interactions in the two fixed-effects models in table 5.1. This is done to separate marginal effects of the interacting variables from each other (Brambor et al. 2006; Craw 2008; Dawson and Richter 2006). This separation also facilitates testing of various interactive hypotheses: whether differences in marginal effects and marginal predictions reported at different combinations of specific values of the moderating variables are different from zero. Bonferroni adjusted standard errors are applied in this regard (Dawson and Richter 2006).

Table 5.4   Significance of Differences in Marginal Effects of School District Competition Log of Per-Pupil Spending Across School Districts Grouped by Political Institutions (Fixed-Effects Model Using Student Enrollment-Weighted Count of School Districts in an MSA)

Marginal Effects of School District Competition Across School Districts Grouped by Political Institutions[a]	dy/dx Contrast	Bonferroni P-Value
Ward DB - Appointed DB	0.608	0.034
Mixed DB - Appointed DB	0.527	0.090
Ward DB - At-Large DB	0.212	0.000

Source: Author's own calculations and tabulation.
[a] Marginal Effect of Student Enrollment-Weighted Count of School Districts is negative and statistically significant for school districts with appointed boards only (b = −0.830; p=0.033). For other school districts grouped by different types of district boards, the marginal effects of Student Enrollment-Weighted Count of School Districts are negative but statistically not significant.

Table 5.5   Significance of Differences in Marginal Predictions of Log of Per-Pupil Spending Across School Districts Grouped by Type of Local Political Institutions and Level of School District Competition (Fixed-Effects Model Using Student Enrollment-Weighted Count of School Districts in an MSA)

Marginal Predictions of Log of Per-Pupil Spending Across School Districts Grouped by Type of Local Political Institutions and Level of School District Competition	Contrast	Bonferroni P-Values
Ward DB & Low Competition - At-Large DB & Low Competition	−0.041	0.024

Source: Author's own calculations and tabulation.
Note: Bonferroni P-Values used to avoid Type-I Error (Rejecting the true null hypothesis).

Results from marginal analyses for interactions in the fixed-effects model that uses the Herfindahl index as the measure for interschool district competition are not presented because none of the comparisons for marginal predictions of log of per-pupil spending across school districts, which are grouped by type of local political institutions and median household income rankings, are significant when P-values are Bonferroni adjusted, except for those in the main results in table 5.1.

Results in tables 5.1, 5.4, and 5.5 show that school districts with ward-based and mixed district boards spend more than those with appointed boards as interschool district competition increases. Similarly, school districts with ward-based district boards spend more than those with at-large boards. These results are consistent with expected relations under the reformism perspective. Table 5.5 presents differences in marginal effects of student enrollment-weighted count of school districts in an MA for all possible comparisons across different types of school boards. The results are presented only for either significant or marginally significant comparisons. As is evident from the relevant fixed-effects model in table 5.1, school districts with ward-based and mixed boards spend significantly more than those with appointed boards with an increase in interschool district competition. Table 5.5 additionally demonstrates that school districts with ward-based boards spend more than those with at-large boards as interschool district competition increases. However, the student enrollment-weighted count of school districts in an MA is statistically significant for school districts with appointed boards only.

Table 5.5 presents statistically significant results for differences in marginal predictions of log of per-pupil total expenditure for all the possible comparisons between school districts that are grouped by different types of school district boards and different levels of interschool district competition. The levels of interschool district competition have been defined as low if the value of the competition measure is about one standard deviation below its weighted mean. The weighted mean for the measure defines the average competition. School district competition is designated as high if the value for the measure is about one standard deviation above its weighted mean. The statistical significance of the sole comparison reveals that in the fixed-effects interactive model with student enrollment-weighted count of school districts in an MA as the measure for interschool district competition, among school districts with low competition those with ward-based boards significantly spend less than those with at-large boards.

Tables 5.1 and 5.6 also present the equity effects of interschool district competition and the type of school district board. It is apparent from looking first at school districts in third and fourth (second highest) income quintile groups in table 5.1 that districts with at-large and mixed boards spend less than those with appointed boards. In the second income quintile group, school

Table 5.6   Significance of Differences in Marginal Predictions of Log of Per-Pupil Total Spending Across School Districts Grouped by Type of Local Political Institutions and Median Household Income Rankings (Fixed-Effects Model Using Student Enrollment-Weighted Count of School Districts in an MSA)

Differences in Marginal Predictions of Log of Per-Pupil Spending Across School Districts Grouped by Type of Local Political Institutions and Median Household Income Rankings	Contrast	Bonferroni P-Values
Appointed & 2nd Qntl - Appointed & Lowest Qntl	0.224	0.031

Source: Author's own calculations and tabulation.

districts with ward-based boards spend significantly less than those with appointed boards. Table 5.1 shows similar results for the fixed-effects model that uses student enrollment-weighted count of school districts in an MA as a measure for interschool district competition, except for school districts with mixed boards. The mixed school district boards in all income quintiles do not significantly spend any different dollars than their counterparts with appointed boards in comparable income quintile groups. Additionally, table 5.6 shows that school districts with appointed boards in the second income quintile group spend more than school districts with appointed boards in the lowest income quintile group. All other possible comparisons are not statistically different from zero, and therefore they are not presented in table 5.6 for parsimony.

Tables 5.7, 5.8, and 5.9 present results for the marginal analyses of the interactions in the two fixed-effects and one instrumental variable fixed-effects models in table 5.2. The results for interactions in the two fixed-effects models in table 5.2 show that school districts with elected superintendents spend significantly more in comparison to those with appointed superintendents for all income quintile groups. Results for the instrumental variable fixed-effects model that uses the Herfindahl index as a measure for interschool district competition are similar except that there is no significant difference in spending by school districts with elected and those with appointed superintendents in the second-lowest income quintiles.

Table 5.7 reports some additional differences in marginal predictions of log of per-pupil total expenditure across school districts that are grouped by the type of superintendent's office and median household income ranking quintiles for one of the fixed-effects models in table 5.2. The fixed-effects model in question uses Herfindahl index as a measure for interschool district competition. The results are presented only for either significant or marginally significant comparisons from among all possible comparisons. Results in table 5.7 show that school districts with elected superintendents in the top two income quintiles spend significantly more than those with appointed superintendents in the two lower-income quintiles.

Table 5.7 Significance of Differences in Marginal Predictions of Log of Per-Pupil Spending Across School Districts Grouped by Type of Local Political Institutions and Median Household Income Rankings (Fixed-Effects Model Using Herfindahl Index in an MSA)

Differences in Marginal Predictions of Log of Per-Pupil Spending Across School Districts Grouped by Type of Local Political Institutions and Median Household Income Rankings	Contrast	Bonferroni P-Value
Elected Superintendent & Top Quintile - Appointed Superintendent & Top Quintile	0.088	0.062

Source: Author's own calculations and tabulation.

Table 5.8 Significance of Differences in Marginal Predictions of Log of Per-Pupil Spending Across School Districts Grouped by Type of Local Political Institutions and Median Household Income Rankings (Fixed-Effects Model Using Student Enrollment-Weighted Count of School Districts in an MSA)

Differences in Marginal Predictions of Log of Per-Pupil Spending Across School Districts Grouped by Type of Local Political Institutions and Median Household Income Rankings	Contrast	Bonferroni P-Value
Elected Superintendent & 2nd Quintile - Elected Superintendent & Bottom Quintile	0.220	0.008
Elected Superintendent & Top Quintile - Appointed Superintendent & Top Quintile	0.089	0.046

Source: Author's own calculations and tabulation.

Table 5.8 reports additional differences in marginal predictions of log of per-pupil total expenditure across school districts that are formed by the type of superintendent's office and median household income ranking quintiles for the other fixed-effects model in table 5.2. The fixed-effects model in question uses student enrollment-weighted count of school districts in an MA as a measure for interschool district competition. The results are presented only for either significant or marginally significant comparisons from among all possible comparisons.

The results in table 5.8 provide partial support for the reformism perspective in terms of school district spending because school districts with elected superintendents in the top income quintile group spend more than school districts with appointed superintendents in the same quintile.

Table 5.9 reports additional differences in marginal predictions of log of per-pupil total expenditure across school districts that are grouped by the type of superintendent's office and median household income ranking quintiles for the instrumental variable fixed-effects model in table 5.2. The model in question uses Herfindahl index as a measure for interschool district competition.

Table 5.9 Significance of Differences in Marginal Predictions of Log of Per-Pupil Spending Across School Districts Grouped by Type of Local Political Institutions and Median Household Income Rankings (Fixed-Effects Instrumental Variable Model Using Herfindahl Index in an MSA)

Differences in Marginal Predictions of Log of Per-Pupil Spending Across School Districts Grouped by Type of Local Political Institutions and Median Household Income Rankings	Contrast	Bonferroni P-Value
Elected Superintendent & Top Quintile - Elected Superintendent & 4th Quintile	0.153	0.001
Elected Superintendent & Top Quintile - Elected Superintendent & 3rd Quintile	0.263	0.000
Elected Superintendent & Top Quintile - Elected Superintendent & 2nd Quintile	0.311	0.038
Elected Superintendent & Top Quintile - Elected Superintendent & Bottom Quintile	0.542	0.000
Elected Superintendent & 4th Quintile - Elected Superintendent & Bottom Quintile	0.389	0.000
Elected Superintendent & 3rd Quintile - Elected Superintendent & Bottom Quintile	0.280	0.000
Elected Superintendent & 2nd Quintile - Elected Superintendent & Bottom Quintile	0.232	0.096
Appointed Superintendent & Top Quintile - Appointed Superintendent & 4th Quintile	0.154	0.000
Appointed Superintendent & Top Quintile - Appointed Superintendent & 3rd Quintile	0.244	0.000
Appointed Superintendent & Top Quintile - Appointed Superintendent & 2nd Quintile	0.334	0.001
Appointed Superintendent & Top Quintile - Appointed Superintendent & Bottom Quintile	0.446	0.000
Appointed Superintendent & 4th Quintile - Appointed Superintendent & Bottom Quintile	0.291	0.000
Appointed Superintendent & 3rd Quintile - Appointed Superintendent & Bottom Quintile	0.202	0.000
Elected Superintendent & 4th Quintile - Appointed Superintendent & 4th Quintile	0.076	0.051

Source: Author's own calculations and tabulation.

The results are presented only for either significant or marginally significant comparisons from among all possible comparisons.

These results illustrate that the extent of inequity in school district spending is slightly higher in school districts with elected superintendents than those with appointed superintendents. This is evident because school districts with elected superintendents in all income quintiles demonstrate inequity in school district spending, whereas the school districts with appointed superintendents in all income quintiles except those in the second income quintile show similar patterns. Appointed superintendents help with equity when the focus is on poorer school districts. The school districts with appointed superintendents are more equitable perhaps because they are better able to manage cooperation with other school districts in providing public education. Frederickson (1999) and LeRoux et al. (2010) argue that professional managers are more adept in brokering and maintaining cooperative service arrangements across local government boundaries than elected officials, who have a shorter time horizon and may be averse to the electoral consequences of cooperation. This finding is consistent with expected relationships under the Tamed Leviathan perspective.

Table 5.9 also provides partial support for the reformism perspective in terms of school district spending because school districts with elected superintendents in the fourth income quintile group spend more than school districts with appointed superintendents in the same quintile.

Tables 5.10 and 5.11 present results for the marginal analyses of the interactions in the random-effects model in table 5.3 that uses student enrollment-weighted count of school districts in an MA as the measure for interschool

Table 5.10 Significance of Differences in Marginal Effects of School District Competition on Log of Per-Pupil Spending Across School Districts Grouped by Political Institutions (Random-Effects Model Using Student Enrollment-Weighted Count of School Districts in an MSA)

Marginal Effects of School District Competition on Log of Per-Pupil Spending Across School Districts Grouped by Political Institutions	dy/dx Contrast	Unadjusted P-Value
Fiscally Dependent School District - Fiscally Independent School District [a]	−0.460	0.017

Source: Author's own calculations and tabulation.
[a] Student Enrollment-Weighted Count of School Districts in an MSA has positive and nonsignificant effect (b=0.053; p=0.533) for independent school districts. For dependent school districts, Student Enrollment-Weighted Count of School Districts in an MSA has negative and significant effect (b = −0.406; p=0.031).

Table 5.11 Significance of differences in Marginal Predictions of Log of Per-Pupil Spending Across School Districts Grouped by Type of Local Political Institutions and Levels of School District Competition (Random-Effects Model Using Student Enrollment-Weighted Count of School Districts in an MSA)

Differences in Marginal Predictions of Log of Per-Pupil Spending Across School Districts Grouped by Type of Local Political Institutions and Levels of School District Competition	Contrast	Bonferroni P-Value
Dependent SD & Average Competition - Independent SD & Average Competition	−0.111	0.008
Dependent SD & High Competition - Independent SD & High Competition	−0.167	0.000

Source: Author's own calculations and tabulation.

district competition. Results in tables 5.3 and 5.10 show that the gap in spending between fiscally dependent and fiscally independent school districts for increasing interschool district competition from 0 (no competition) to 1 (perfect competition) is about 46 percent lower for the former type of school districts. However, as shown in the notes below table 5.10, the interschool district competition has a significantly negative effect for the fiscally dependent school districts spending only.

Table 5.11 additionally breaks down this interaction by presenting statistically significant results for differences in marginal predictions of log of per-pupil total expenditure for all the possible comparisons between school districts that are grouped by different types of fiscal autonomy and different levels of interschool district competition. The statistically significant comparisons reveal that in the random-effects interactive model with student enrollment-weighted count of school districts in an MA as the measure for interschool district competition, fiscally dependent school districts in the average and high competition groups spend less than fiscally independent school districts in average and high competition groups, respectively. This finding confirms the expected relationship under the Extended Tamed Leviathan hypothesis.

DISCUSSION OF THE KEY FINDINGS

Marginal analyses of the significant interaction effects show that the increase in interschool district competition leads to lower school district spending. This result is consistent with hypotheses under the public choice and the Leviathan models. However, the nonsignificance of interaction terms and the significance of main effects in other relevant fixed-effects models imply that the increase in interschool district competition leads to higher school district spending. Substantively, this result is consistent with the consolidated local governments' model. Similar to the corresponding results in the additive models, these results together suggest that interschool district competition does not robustly affect school district spending.

Similar to the variation in marginal effects of interschool district competition with different types of local political institutions, results of the variation in the marginal effects of local political institutions at different levels of interschool district competition are presented. Unlike the additive models, marginal analyses of these interactions show that local political institutions do not conclusively affect school district spending. Among school districts with low competition in the fixed-effects interactive model with student enrollment-weighted count of school districts in an MA as the measure for interschool district competition, those with ward-based boards spend significantly less than those with at-large boards. This finding fails to support the efficiency argument in the reformism model concerning the presence of fewer incentives for at-large elected local representatives than ward-based elected local representatives for inflating public budgets to win votes and allies. Additionally, in the random-effects interactive model where student enrollment-weighted count of school districts in an MA is the measure of interschool district competition, fiscally dependent school districts in the average and high competition groups spend less than fiscally independent school districts in these groups. This result implies that if school districts are either an arm of other local governments or fully dependent on state governments, they reap the benefits from economies of scale and hence spend less than independent school districts. This finding supports the extended Tamed Leviathan Model and the consolidated local governments' models.

The interactive models also show the effects of interschool district competition and local political institutions on equity in school district spending. The nonsignificance of the interactions between interschool district competition and within-state median household income rankings of school districts shows that interschool district competition does not influence equity in school district spending. This finding does not support the relevant hypothesis in the consolidated local governments' model. This absence of equity implications may partly stem from the fact that court-ordered school finance reform has more than proportionately increased spending in lower-income school districts in comparison to those in higher-income groups (Baker 2018; Harris et al. 2001; Murray et al. 1998).

However, the type of local political institutions does have equity implications for school district spending. For example, with few exceptions, school districts with appointed boards spend more than their counterparts in similar income quintile groups. The results in regard to the type of school district superintendent suggest that the extent of inequity in school district spending is slightly higher in school districts with elected superintendents than those with appointed superintendents. School districts with professional officials are more equitable perhaps because they are better able to manage cooperation with other school districts in providing public education. Frederickson (1999) and LeRoux et al. (2010) argue that professional managers are more adept in brokering and maintaining cooperative service arrangements across local government boundaries than elected officials, who have a shorter time horizon and may be averse to the electoral consequences of cooperation. These results partially support the reformism perspective in terms of school district spending.

Overall, the findings robustly support the equity effects of the type of local political institutions. School districts with relatively more professional political institutions are also more equitable. The additive models, the interactive

models, and the marginal analyses support the reformism model, the extended
Tamed Leviathan Model, and the consolidated local governments' models to
some extent. With an increase in competition, school districts with relatively
more professional political institutions spend less. Dependent school districts
reap the benefits from economies of scale, and hence spend less than independent school districts. Interschool district competition does not lead to inequity
in spending.

NOTES

1. The UFNFD data has been utilized over the FNFD data because of three reasons. First, the majority of school districts in the United States are unified. And the
unified K-12 "pseudo-district" in the UFNFD data addresses the methodological
challenge in analyzing school districts in different grade spans separately. Many
measures, such as mean per-pupil expenditures, are different for districts with different grade spans (Williams et al. 2006). The school districts in the secondary grade
span typically spend higher dollars than school districts with elementary grade spans
(Hussar and Sonnenberg 2000, p. 7). Williams et al. (2006, p. 8) note that "analyses
that attempt to estimate the relation between expenditures and other school characteristics will be distorted when they compare school districts, ignoring the elementary/
secondary differential." The authors further add that for avoiding these biases, "such
comparisons should be carried out using the UFNFD file of unified K–12 pseudo-
districts" because the creation of unified K-12 "pseudo-districts" results in fiscal
and nonfiscal measures that are comparable to those for the majority unified regular
districts in the United States. Williams et al. (2006, p. 8) suggest that "studies that
aim to compare school districts in a randomly selected sample will benefit from the
availability of the unified K-12 pseudo-district UFNFD file as a sampling frame: per
pupil revenues and expenditures, student characteristics, and outcomes can be compared across similarly situated districts or district clusters (i.e., pseudo-districts)."
Second, keeping elementary districts separate from secondary school districts to
which students from the former transfer after leaving elementary grades would result
in upward bias in measuring inter-school district competition. This is so because
the separate secondary district is dependent on the former for students rather than
competing for students with them. Finally, although similar to the FNFD data, the
UFNFD data flags outlier values for closer scrutiny of by researchers because not all
outlier values are necessarily wrong (Williams et al. 2006). In this book's sample,
16 school districts were flagged as outliers for just a single year each on per-pupil
expenditure and other fiscal variables. I replaced such values with values from most
adjacent year (within the study period) that were not considered outliers for each
school district. Such replacement values were not themselves outliers because they
were either not more than 3 standard deviations from the mean of the other years for
any given LEA or not different by a factor of 1.5 in either direction from a preceding
year for any given LEA (Williams et al. 2006).

2. In the regression models, the sample size reduces by about 15 percent for the pooled OLS and fixed-effects models and by about 21 percent for the instrumental variable fixed-effects models because of missing observations for variables in estimation models.

3. For avoiding estimation bias, Hoxby (2000) and Rothstein (2007) utilize the number of larger and smaller streams in a Metropolitan Area as instruments for interschool district competition in linear models on cross-section data. This chapter does not use these instruments for interschool district competition measures because they are time-invariant and therefore they are collinear with unobserved time-invariant school district-level factors. Consequently, they will fail to identify an unbiased coefficient for the latter in the fixed-effects model setting.

4. The instrumental variable fixed-effects command in STATA does not permit the use of weights; therefore, fixed-effects IV models are not weighted.

5. The corresponding interactive model shows similar results.

Chapter 6

Conclusions and Policy Implications

This book studies interrelated questions concerning the policy implications of equity in provisioning of K-12 public education by filling several gaps in the relevant theoretical and empirical literature. In addressing these gaps, this book focuses on the role of school district-level locational factors including interschool district competition and the type of political institutions in school district spending. The book focuses on equity in school spending in the context of major reforms and debates before venturing into the study of these relationships by combining and extending the extant theoretical traditions in a novel way. This synthesis of the extant literature on efficiency and equity implications of interschool district competition provides a conceptual model that entails empirical estimation of the interactive effects of political institutions with interschool district competition on provisioning of public education. Provisioning of public education has not been studied along this line before.

There is limited research on the role of school choice, defined as interschool district competition, on unequal school district spending. The broader view in the literature on school choice is that market-like competition for students would nudge public schools toward productive efficiency in resource use and better educational outcomes (Belfield and Levin 2005b; Chubb and Moe 1990; Gill and Booker 2015; Godwin and Kemerer 2002). Critics of school choice find such policies inequitable and inefficient. The few studies on the effects of interschool district competition on school district spending offer inconclusive empirical evidence (Hoxby 2000; Rothstein 2007). Therefore, an empirical investigation of the role of school choice defined as interschool district competition is important and has policy relevance.

Similarly, an investigation of the role of political institutions in spending and student learning is important because existing studies ignore the role of political institutions in the equity of school district spending. Political institutions are important to consider while investigating equity in spending because the local political institutions influence local taxation and spending (Craw 2008; Feiock et al. 2003). As local residents' political representatives, political institutions also match citizen demand with school district spending (Berkman and Plutzer 2005).

The questions about inequity in provisioning have received significant policy attention during past several decades. Since the landmark decision in *Serrano v. Priest* in 1971 in California and the famous US Supreme Court's judgment in *Rodriguez v. San Antonio* in 1973, there has been a great deal of activism on the part of the judiciary, states, and civil society actors in attaining the goal of equitable provisioning of public education among school districts in the United States. The funding of public schools is a very important issue because it consumes a major portion of resources of the state and school districts in the United States. In spite of several decades of effort at addressing inequity in education financing, the problem still persists, though to a lesser extent than in the past (Baker 2018). From the public policy perspective, therefore, it is very important to list out the factors that explain this inequity in provisioning. The findings on the interactive effects of interschool district competition and political institution on spending levels inform the policymakers in regard to bringing appropriate institutional and political changes for more equitable and better outcomes. Furthermore, since public education is a de facto public good, the political institutions of the local school districts and state governments should be made aware of the most appropriate ways of translating public preferences into spending levels. In such an endeavor, spending behavior of different types of political institutions of local governments plays an important role. This book attempts to disentangle the most important factors that explain inequitable provisioning in the school districts across the United States. This goal is achieved by examining the roles of political institutions and interschool district competition on differential spending by school districts in different within-state income quintiles in the United States after controlling for a number of other relevant factors.

Specifically, the interactive effects of political institutions and interschool district competition in an MA on school district's spending are examined, in general, and equity in school district's spending, in particular. The equity effects of political institutions and interschool district competition on school district spending are examined by separately testing their interactions with school districts' within-state median household income rankings. The empirical investigation of these interactive hypotheses is situated within the purview of the Extended Tamed Leviathan model that integrates several topical theories, including the public choice, the Leviathan, the consolidated local

governments, the reformism, the Tamed Leviathan, and the policy responsiveness models.

The Extended Tamed Leviathan model accomplishes this integration by
formulating hypotheses in opposite direction to the key arguments in the
Tamed Leviathan and the consolidated local governments' models because
the two models predict opposing effects of interlocal competition/decen-
tralization on local government spending. The theoretical argument in the
Extended Tamed Leviathan model is that the consolidation of government
between suburban regions and inner-cities provides economies of scale. Such
local governments can also efficiently and equitably manage spillovers from
interdependent localities. However, some forms of political institutions may
cater to narrower constituency needs, and hence may spend higher dollars
even when there is less decentralization. Conversely, the Tamed Leviathan
model argues that with fewer options to relocate to other local jurisdictions,
the residents can be taxed at higher rates for a given level of public good.
However, some forms of political institutions can objectively take broader
constituency perspective and spend fewer dollars even when there is less
decentralization.

Prior studies have not considered these interactive effects in the contexts of
school district spending in the United States and the Extended Tamed Leviathan model. For examining these hypotheses, a unique longitudinal dataset
has been constructed by combining relevant datasets from several sources.
Fixed-effects and instrumental variable fixed-effects regression models are
employed to handle the endogeneity problem in most econometric studies
(Cameron and Trivedi 2009) and several policy evaluation studies that utilize
nonexperimental data (see, for example, Harris et al. 2001; Bettinger 2005).

School choice in terms of home schooling, private schools, and residential
choice has always existed. Some scholars favor residential choice, while
others find it inequitable and inefficient in public education. School choice
reform creates market-type schools so that parents have more choice and
schools have autonomy. Several scholars propose that through program
design, school choice programs can protect inner-city students from disadvantages on account of ethnicity and socioeconomic status (SES). Critics of
school choice find such policies inequitable and inefficient. In recent decades,
more market-like schools in the form of charter schools, vouchers, and magnet schools have come up. However, there is no conclusive evidence of the
positive effects of such reform policies. In fact, empirical evidence suggests
that these policies have led to resegregation. Also, the theoretical and empirical literatures have not conclusively established the supremacy of school
choice policies over the traditional public education system. This book looks
at this debate afresh in the context of the school choice in the form interschool
district competition. Specifically, the empirical estimation evaluates the

interactive effects of political institutions with interschool district competition on equity in school district spending.

This book offers several interesting findings. In regard to school district spending, the results show that interschool district competition does not robustly affect school district spending. Results also show that local political institutions do not conclusively affect the level of school district spending. School districts with ward-based and mixed boards spend more than those with appointed boards as the level of interschool district competition increases. These results are consistent with the reformism and the Tamed Leviathan models. However, results show that the type of school district board with seemingly less incentive for inflating public budgets to win votes and allies such as the at-large district boards actually spend more than ward-based school district boards that arguably have more incentive to spend. These findings provide some evidence against the reformism perspective. Results also show that school districts that are either an arm of other local governments or fully dependent on state governments reap the benefits from economies of scale and hence spend lower amounts than fiscally independent school districts. This finding supports the consolidated local government model. Additionally, the Tamed Leviathan hypothesis is supported because accountability to parent local government restricts the ability of fiscally dependent districts from inflating budgets for rent-seeking.

The absence of evidence for interaction between interschool district competition and median household income rankings implies that interschool district competition does not lead to inequity in spending by school districts in different income quintiles. This result is not surprising because there is not enough support for the general overall effects of interschool district competition in both additive and interactive models. This finding does not support the relevant hypothesis in the consolidated local governments' model. This absence of equity implications may be due to the fact that court-ordered school finance reform has resulted in relatively higher spending in lower-income school districts in comparison to upper-income school districts (Harris et al. 2001; Murray et al. 1998).

In respect of equity effects of different types of political institutions on school district spending, results show that with few exceptions, school districts with appointed boards are more equitable in spending than their counterparts in similar income quintile groups. Similarly results show that the extent of inequity in spending is more pronounced for school districts with elected superintendents. School districts with professional officials are more equitable perhaps because they are better able to manage cooperation with other school districts in providing public education. Frederickson (1999) and LeRoux et al. (2010) argue that professional managers are more adept in brokering and maintaining cooperative service arrangements across local government boundaries than elected officials, who have a shorter time horizon and may be averse to the electoral consequences of cooperation. These results partially support the reformism perspective in terms of school district spending.

Overall, the findings in regard to school district spending robustly support the equity effects of the type of local political institutions. School districts with relatively more professional political institutions are also more equitable. The additive models, the interactive models, and the marginal analyses support the reformism model, the Extended Tamed Leviathan Model, and the consolidated local governments' models to some extent. With an increase in competition school districts with relatively more professional political institutions spend less. Dependent school districts reap the benefits from economies of scale and hence spend less than independent school districts. Interschool district competition does not lead to inequity in spending.

An adequate understanding of the regional and local contexts such as the roles of the levels of interschool district competition and types of local political institutions in equity in school district spending and equity and productive efficiency in educational outcomes helps policymakers adapt policies to those contexts. The empirical findings in this book clarify why and how organizational, socioeconomic, and political contexts matter in bringing desirable educational outcomes. Policymakers can bring commensurate changes in the organizational and political setup of school districts for achieving the goal of more equitable and effective public education. From a public policy perspective, findings of this book therefore inform the formulation of appropriate policies for better educational outcomes through reorganization of school finance.

The findings of this book suggest that if policymakers intend to address inequity in spending across school districts without raising the level of spending, then they might consider having more professional political institutions such as appointed boards in school districts as one of the policy solutions. Additionally, in achieving this policy goal, policymakers needn't worry about the degree of interschool district competition in metropolitan areas because it neither affects the level of spending nor inequity in spending among school districts.

There are however a few data and methodological limitations of this book. The Census Bureau has stopped collecting data on local political institutions in years subsequent to the year 1992 when such data were collected last. The results from the random-effects models for the fiscally dependent districts are indicative because the fixed-effects models are more appropriate. However, the latter did not identify the coefficient for the fiscally dependent school districts, so the random-effects model was used instead.

Apart from the methodological issues, the policy suggestions from this book entail support from important local political constituents with varying political interests in public education including parents with children, old-age population, and inner-city residents. Local school district governments may face a situation in which the old-age population is less supportive of higher spending on public education (Poterba 1997; Harris et al. 2001) because they may believe that families with school-age children receive nearly all of the benefits from spending on public schools. However, Harris et al. (2001) offer a number of reasons why the elderly might support public education. One, the old-age population may expect to receive higher revenue for Social Security and Medicare from taxing higher wages of younger workers. This economic scenario becomes possible because higher investment in public education improves workers' skills and productivity that ultimately result in higher wages. Two, the elderly may simply believe in philanthropy when it comes to public education. Three, elderly homeowners may hold the expectation that higher spending on education will be capitalized into the value of their homes. Four, Tiebout sorting by the elderly could leave education spending unchanged because they may simply choose to live in districts with low education spending. Finally, the elderly may have higher interests in reducing crime rates and increasing economic activities. In achieving these goals, the elderly may support public education because public schools socialize children, giving them an understanding of civic duties, social norms, and regular work habits.

Since having more professional political institutions is good for equity in spending, the elderly may support this policy option. Although the elderly may prefer more school districts within their metropolitan area for raising general skills and educational outcomes of younger generation in public schools, they might also prefer to achieve some balance in equity and productive efficiency.

Since parents with school-age children have real interest in supporting public education with better educational outcomes, the other important local interest group that influences local educational policy comprises inner-city residents. Unlike the elderly, the inner-city residents do not possess the wherewithal to exercise the Tiebout residential choice. In fact, they bear the brunt of several bad policy consequences of Tiebout competition. However, similar to the elderly, it is in economic interests of inner-city residents to support policy options for equitable public education spending.

References

Aaronson, Daniel, Barrow, Lisa, and Sander, William. "Teachers and Student Achievement in the Chicago Public High Schools." *Journal of Labor Economics*, 25(1) (2007): 95–135.

Ahmed, S., and Greene, K. V. "Is the Median Voter a Clear-Cut Winner? Comparing the Median Voter Theory and Competing Theories in Explaining Local Government Spending." *Public Choice*, 105 (2000): 207–30.

Almeida, T. A. "Refocusing School Finance Litigation On At-Risk Children: Leandro v. State of North Carolina." *Yale Law & Policy Review*, 22(2) (2004): 525–69.

Altshuler, A., Morrill, W., Wolman, H., and Mitchell, F. (eds.). *Governance and Opportunity in Metropolitan America*. Washington, DC: National Academy Press, 1999.

Andrews, M., Duncombe, W. D., and Yinger, J. "Revisiting Economies of Size in American Education: Are We Any Closer to a Consensus?" *Economics of Education Review*, 21 (2002): 245–62.

Anyon, J. *Radical Possibilities: Public Policy, Urban Education, and a New Social Movement*. New York: Routledge, 2005.

Baker, B. D. *Educational Inequality and School Finance: Why Money Matters for America's Students*. Cambridge, MA: Harvard Education Press, 2018.

Baker, B. D., and Green, P. C. "Conceptions of Equity and Adequacy in School Finance." In *Handbook of Research in Education Finance and Policy*, edited by H. F. Ladd and Edward B. Fiske (pp. 247–59). New York: Routledge, 2015.

Baker, B. D., and Weber, M. *Deconstructing the Myth of American Public Schooling Inefficiency*. Albert Shanker Institute, 2016.

Bayer, P., and Timmins, C. "Estimating Equilibrium Models of Sorting Across Locations." *Economic Journal*, 117(518) (2007): 353–74.

Belfield, C. R., and Levin, H. M. "Vouchers and Public Policy: When Ideology Trumps Evidence." *American Journal of Education*, 11 (2005a): 548–67.

Belfield, C. R., and Levin, H. M. *Privatizing Educational Choice: Consequences for Parents, Schools, and Public Policy*. Boulder, CO: Paradigm Publishers, 2005b.

Bergstrom, T. C., and Goodman, R. P. "Private Demands for Public Goods." *American Economic Review*, 63 (1973): 280–96.

Berkman, M. B., and Plutzer, E. *Ten Thousand Democracies: Politics and Public Opinion in America's School Districts*. Washington, DC: Georgetown University Press, 2005.

Berry, C. "Piling On: The Fiscal Effects of Jurisdictional Overlap." *American Journal of Political Science*, 52 (2008): 802–20.

Berry, C. "The Impact of School Finance Judgments on State Fiscal Policy." In *School Money Trials: The Legal Pursuit of Educational Adequacy*, edited by Martin R. West and Paul E. Peterson (pp. 213–42). Washington, DC: Brookings Institution Press, 2007.

Berry, C. R. "School District Consolidation and Student Outcomes: Does Size Matter?" In *Besieged: School Boards and the Future of Education Politics*, edited by H. G. Howell (pp. 56–80). Washington, DC: The Brookings Institution, 2005.

Berry, C. R., and Gersen, J. E. "Fiscal Consequences of Electoral Institutions." *Journal of Law and Economics*, 52(3) (2009): 469–95.

Berry, C. R., and West, M. R. "Growing Pains: The School Consolidation Movement and Student Outcomes." *The Journal of Law, Economics, & Organization*, 26(1) (2010): 1–29.

Bettinger, E. P. "The Effect of Charter Schools on Charter Students and Public Schools." *Economics of Education Review*, 24 (2005): 133–47.

Betts, J. R., and Loveless, T. (eds.). *Getting Choice Right: Ensuring Equity and Efficiency in Education Policy*. Washington, DC: Brookings Institution Press, 2005.

Bifulco, R., and Bulkley, K. "Charter Schools." In *Handbook of Research in Education Finance and Policy*, edited by H. F. Ladd and Edward B. Fiske (pp. 439–59). New York: Routledge, 2015.

Borcherding, T. E., and Deacon, R. T. "The Demand for the Services of Non-Federal Governments." *American Economic Review*, 62 (1972): 891–901.

Borman, Geoffrey, and Maritza Dowling, N. "Schools and Inequality: A Multilevel Analysis of Coleman's Equality of Educational Opportunity Data." *Teachers College Record*, 112(5) (2010): 1201–46.

Boyd, D., Lankford, H., Loeb, S., and Wyckoff, J. "The Draw of Home: How Teachers' Preferences for Proximity Disadvantage Urban Schools." *Journal of Policy Analysis and Management*, 24(1) (2005): 113–32.

Boyne, G. A. "Local Government Structure and Performance: Lessons from America." *Public Administration*, 70 (1992a): 333–57.

Boyne, G. A. "Is There a Relationship between Fragmentation and Local Government Cost?" *Urban Affairs Quarterly*, 28 (1992b): 317–22.

Brambor, T., Clark, W. R., and Golder, M. "Understanding Interaction Models: Improving Empirical Analyses." *Political Analysis*, 14(1) (2006): 63–82.

Brennan, G., and Buchanan, J. *The Power to Tax: Analytic Foundations of a Fiscal Constitution*. Cambridge: Cambridge University Press, 1980.

Burns, N. *The Formation of American Local Governments: Private Values in Public Institutions*. New York: Oxford University Press, 1994.

Burtless, G. *Does Money Matter? The Effect of School Resources on Student Achievement and Adult Success*. Washington, DC: The Brookings Institution, 1996.

Cameron, A. C., and Trivedi, P. K. *Microeconometrics using Stata* (Vol. 5). College Station, TX: Stata Press, 2009.

Campbell, R. J. "Leviathan and Fiscal Illusion in Local Government Overlapping Jurisdictions." *Public Choice*, 120(3–4) (2004): 301–29.

Carony, M., and Loeb, S. "Does External Accountability Affect Student Outcome?" *Education Evaluation and Policy Analysis*, 24(4) (2002): 305–31.

Carnoy, M., and Rothstein, R. "What Do International Tests Really Show about US Student Performance." *Economic Policy Institute*, 28 (2013): 32–33.

Carruthers, J. I. "Growth at the Fringe: The Impact of Political Fragmentation in United States Metropolitan Areas." *Papers in Regional Science*, 82 (2003): 475–99.

Carruthers, J. I., and Ulfarsson, G. F. "Fragmentation and Sprawl: Evidence from Interregional Analysis." *Growth and Change*, 33(3) (2002): 312–40.

Chemerinsky, E. "Separate and Unequal: American Public Education Today." *American University Law Review*, 52(6) (2003): 1461–75.

Chubb, J. E., and Moe, T. M. *Politics, Markets, and America's Schools*. Washington, DC: Brookings Institution, 1990.

Chubb, J. E., and Moe, T. M. "Politics, Markets and the Organization of Schools." *American Political Science Review*, 82(4) (1988): 1065–87.

Cnudde, C. F. "Book Reviews: American Politics – Ten Thousand Democracies: Politics and Public Opinion in American School Districts." *Perspectives on Politics*, 4(3) (2006): 587–88.

Coleman, J., Campbell, E., Hobson, C., McPartland, J., Mood, A., and Winfield, F. *Equality of Educational Opportunity*. Washington, DC: U.S. Government Printing Office, 1966.

Condron, D. J. "Social Class, School and Non-School Environments, and Black/White Inequalities in Children's Learning." *American Sociological Review*, 74 (2009): 683–708.

Condron, D., and Roscigno, V. "Disparities Within: Unequal Spending and Achievement in an Urban School District." *Sociology of Education*, 76(1) (2003): 18–33.

Cooley, J. *Desegregation and the Achievement Gap: Do Diverse Peers Help?* Madison: Department of Economics, University of Wisconsin. Unpublished manuscript, 2009.

Coons, J. E., Clune, W. H., and Sugarman, S. D. *Private Wealth and Public Education*. Cambridge, MA: Harvard University Press, 1970.

Corcoran, S. P., and Evans, W. N. "Equity, Adequacy and the Evolving State Role in Education Finance." In *Handbook of Research in Education Finance and Policy*, edited by H. F. Ladd and Edward B. Fiske (p. 332). New York: Routledge, 2008.

Corcoran, S. P., and Evans, W. N. "Equity, Adequacy and the Evolving State Role in Education Finance." In *Handbook of Research in Education Finance and Policy*, edited by H. F. Ladd and Edward B. Fiske (pp. 353–71). New York: Routledge, 2015.

Craw, M. "Taming the Local Leviathan: Institutional and Economic Constraints on Municipal Budgets." *Urban Affairs Review*, 43(5) (2008): 663–90.

Dawson, J. F., and Richter, A. W. "Probing Three-Way Interactions in Moderated Multiple Regression: Development and Application of a Slope Difference Test." *Journal of Applied Psychology*, 91(4) (2006): 917–26.

DeHoog, R. H., Lowery, D., and Lyons, W. E. "Citizen Satisfaction with Local Governance: A Test of Individual, Jurisdictional, and City Specific Explanations." *Journal of Politics*, 52 (1990): 807–37.

Deere, D., and Strayer, W. "Putting Schools to Test: School Accountability, Incentives and Behavior." *Working Paper*, Texas A&M University, 2001.

Dolan, D. A. "Local Government Fragmentation: Does It Drive Up the Cost of Government?" *Urban Affairs Quarterly*, 26(1) (1990): 28–45.

Dowding, K., John, P., and Biggs, S. "Tiebout: A Survey of the Empirical Literature." *Urban Studies*, 31(4–5) (1994): 767–97.

Downes, T. A., and Stiefel, L. "Measuring Equity and Adequacy in School Finance." In *Handbook of Research in Education Finance and Policy*, edited by H. F. Ladd and Edward B. Fiske (pp. 222–37). New York: Routledge, 2015.

Downs, Anthony. *New Visions for Metropolitan America*. Washington, DC: Brookings Institution, 1994.

Dreier, Peter, Mollenkopf, John, and Swanstrom, Todd. *Place Matters: Metropolitics for the Twenty-First Century*. Lawrence: University Press of Kansas, 2001.

Driscoll, D., Halcoussis, D., and Svorny, S. "School District Size and Student Performance." *Economics of Education Review*, 22 (2003): 193–201.

Duncombe, W. "Estimating the Cost of an Adequate Education in New York." *Center for Policy Research Working Paper Number 44*, Syracuse University; Maxwell School of Citizenship and Public Affairs, 2002.

Duncombe, W. D., and Yinger, J. "Measurement of Cost Differentials." In *Handbook of Research in Education Finance and Policy*, edited by H. F. Ladd and Edward B. Fiske (pp. 276–94). New York: Routledge, 2015.

Duncombe, W., and Yinger, J. "Performance Standards and Educational Cost Indices: You Can't Have One without the Other." In *Equity and Adequacy in Education Finance: Issues and Perspectives*, edited by H. Ladd, R. Chalk, and J. Hansen (p. 261). Washington, DC: National Academy Press, 1999.

Duncombe, W., Ruggiero, J., and Yinger, J. "Alternative Approaches to Measuring the Cost of Education." In *Holding Schools Accountable: Performance-Based Reform in Education*, edited by H. F. Ladd (pp. 327–56). Washington, DC: The Brookings Institution, 1996.

Eberts, R. W., and Gronberg, T. J. "Can Competition among Local Governments Constrain Government Spending?" *Federal Reserve Bank of Cleveland Economic Review*, 24(1) (1988): 2–9.

Eberts, R. W., and Gronberg, T. J. "Structure, Conduct, and Performance in the Local Public Sector." *National Tax Journal*, 43(2) (1990): 165–73.

Elliott, Marta. "School Finance and Opportunities to Learn: Does Money Well Spent Enhance Students' Achievement?" *Sociology of Education*, 71(3) (1998): 223–45.

Epple, D., and Romano, R. "Neighborhood Schools, Choice, and the Distribution of Educational Benefits." *NBER Working Paper* (2000): #W7596.

Ericson, D. P. "Liberty and Equality in Education: A Summary Review." *Education Theory*, 34(1) (1984): 97–102.

Evans, W. N., Murray, S. E., and Schwab, R. M. "Schoolhouses, Courthouses, and Statehouses after *Serrano*." *Journal of Policy Analysis and Management*, 16(1) (1997): 10–31.

Farkas, G. "Racial Disparities and Discrimination in Education: What Do We know, How Do We Know It, and What Do We Need to Know?" *Teachers College Record*, 105(6) (2003): 1119–46.

Farnham, P. G. "The Impact of Citizen Influence on Local Government Expenditure." *Public Choice*, 64(3) (1990): 201–12.

Feiock, R. C., Jeong, M.-G., and Kim, J. "Credible Commitment and Council-Manager Government: Implications for Policy Instrument Choices." *Public Administration Review*, 63(5) (2003): 616–25.

Figlio, D. "Testing Crime and Punishment." *Journal of Public Economics*, 90(4–5) (2006): 837–51.

Figlio, D. N., and Ladd, H. F. "School Accountability and Student Achievement." In *Handbook of Research in Education Finance and Policy*, edited by H. F. Ladd and Edward B. Fiske (pp. 166–82). New York: Routledge, 2008.

Figlio, D. N., and Ladd, H. F. "School Accountability and Student Achievement." In *Handbook of Research in Education Finance and Policy*, edited by H. F. Ladd and Edward B. Fiske (pp. 210–25). New York: Routledge, 2015.

Finn, J. D., and Achilles, C. M. "Tennessee's Class Size Study: Findings, Implications, Misconceptions." *Educational Evaluation and Policy Analysis*, 21 (1999): 97–109.

Fischel, W. A. *The Homevoter Hypothesis: How Home Values Influence Local Government Taxation, School Finance and Land Use Policies*. Harvard University Press, 2001.

Fischel, W. A. *Making the Grade: The Economic Evolution of American School Districts*. Chicago: University of Chicago Press, 2009.

Fiske, E., and Ladd, H. F. *When Schools Compete: A Cautionary Tale*. Washington, DC: Brookings Institution, 2000.

Forbes, K. F., and Zampelli, E. M. "Is Leviathan a Mythical Beast?" *American Economic Review*, 79(3) (1989): 568–77.

Foster, K. *Regionalism On Purpose*. Cambridge, MA: Report Prepared for The Lincoln Institute of Land Policy, 2001.

Foster, K. A. *The Political Economy of Special Purpose Governments*. Washington, DC: Georgetown University Press, 1997.

Fox, W. F. "Reviewing Economies of Size in Education." *Journal of Education and Finance*, 6(3) (1981): 273–96.

Frant, H. "High-Powered and Low-Powered Incentives in the Public Sector." *Journal of Public Administration Research and Theory*, 6(3) (1996): 365–81.

Frederickson, H. G. "The Repositioning of American Public Administration." *PS: Political Science and Politics*, 32(4) (1999): 701–11.

Frederickson, H. G., Johnson, G. A., and Wood, C. *The Adapted City: Institutional Dynamics and Structural Change*. Armonk, NY: M.E. Sharpe, 2004.

Friedman, M. "The Role of Government in Education." In *Economics and the Public Interest*, edited by R. Solo (pp. 123–44). New Brunswick, NJ: Rutgers University Press, 1955.

Friedman, Milton. *Capitalism and Freedom*. Chicago: University of Chicago Press, 1962.

Fryer, R. G. Jr., and Levitt, S. D. "Understanding the Black-White Test Score Gap in the First Two Years of School." *Review of Economics and Statistics*, 86(2) (2004): 447–64.

Fryer, R. G. Jr., and Levitt, S. D. "The Black-White Test Score Gap Through the Third Grade." *NBER Working Paper* (2005): #11049.

Fulton, W., Pendall, R., Nguyen, M., and Harrison, A. *Who Sprawls Most? How Growth Patterns Differ across the U.S.* Washington, DC: Brookings Institution, 2001. http://www.brookings.edu/es/urban/publications/fulton.pdf.

Gill, B., and Booker, K. "Student Competition and Student Outcomes." In *Handbook of Research in Education Finance and Policy*, edited by H. F. Ladd and Edward B. Fiske (pp. 183–200). New York: Routledge, 2008.

Gill, B., and Booker, K. "Student Competition and Student Outcomes." In *Handbook of Research in Education Finance and Policy*, edited by H. F. Ladd and Edward B. Fiske (pp. 227–44). New York: Routledge, 2015.

Godwin, R. K., and Kemerer, F. R. *School Choice Tradeoffs: Liberty, Equity, and Diversity*. Austin, TX: University of Texas Press, 2002.

Gordon, N., and Knight, B. "The Effects of School District Consolidation on Educational Cost and Quality." *Public Finance Review*, 36(4) (2008): 408–30.

Gordon, N. E. "The Changing Federal Role in Education Finance and Governance." In *Handbook of Research in Education Finance and Policy*, edited by H. F. Ladd and Edward B. Fiske (pp. 333–51). New York: Routledge, 2015.

Greenwald, R., Hedges, L., and Laine, R. "The Effect of School Resources on School Achievement." *Review of Educational Research*, 66(3) (1996): 361–96.

Grubb, W. N. *The Money Myth: School Resources, Outcomes, and Equity*. New York: Russell Sage Foundation, 2009.

Gujarati, D. N. *Basic Econometrics*. Third International Edition. McGraw-Hill, 1995.

Guthrie, J. W., and Wong, K. K. "The Continually Evolving Political Context of Education Finance." In *Handbook of Research in Education Finance and Policy*, edited by H. F. Ladd and Edward B. Fiske (pp. 76–92). New York: Routledge, 2015.

Hanushek, E. "The Impact of Differential Expenditures on School Performance." *Educational Researcher*, 18(4) (1989a): 45–65.

Hanushek, E. "Throwing Money at Schools." *Journal of Policy Analysis and Management*, 1 (1989b): 19–41.

Hanushek, E. "When School Finance 'Reform' May Not Be Good Policy." *Harvard Journal on Legislation*, 28 (1991): 423–56.

Hanushek, E. "Money Might Matter Somewhere: A Response to Hedges, Laine, and Greenwald." *Educational Researcher*, 23 (1994): 5–8.

Hanushek, E. "A More Complete Picture of School Resource Policies." *Review of Educational Research*, 66 (1996a): 397–409.

Hanushek, E. "School Resources and Student Performance." In *Does Money Matter? The Effect of School Resources on Student Achievement and Adult Success*, edited by G. Burtless (pp. 43–73). Washington, DC: Brookings Institution, 1996b.

Hanushek, E. "Evidence, Politics, and the Class Size Debate." In *The Class Size Debate*, edited by L. Mishel and R. Richards (pp. 37–65). Washington, DC: The Economic Policy Institute, 2002.

Hanushek, E., and Rivkin, S. "Generalizations about Using Valued-Added Measures of Teacher Quality." *American Economic Review*, 100(2) (2010): 267–71.

Hanushek, E. A. "Some Findings from an Independent Investigation of the Tennessee STAR Experiment and from Other Investigations of Class Size Effects." *Educational Evaluation and Policy Analysis*, 21(2) (1999): 143–64.

Hanushek, E. A. "The Alchemy of 'Costing Out' an Adequate Education. Program for Education Policy and Governance." *Working Paper 05–28*, Taubman Center for State and Local Government and Center for American Political Studies, Harvard University, 2005a.

Hanushek, E. A. "Pseudo-Science and a Sound Basic Education: Voodoo Statistics in New York." *Education Next*, 4 (2005b): 67–73.

Hanushek, E. A. (ed.). *Courting Failure: How School Finance Lawsuits Exploit Judges' Good Intentions and Harm Our Children*. Stanford, CA: Education Next Books, 2006.

Hanushek, E. A. "The Alchemy of 'Costing Out' an Adequate Education." In *School Money Trials: The Legal Pursuit of Educational Adequacy*, edited by Martin R. West and Paul E. Peterson (pp. 77–101). Washington, DC: Brookings, 2007a.

Hanushek, E. A. "The Confidence Men: Selling Adequacy: Making Millions." *Education Next*, 7(3) (2007b): 73–78.

Hanushek, E. A., and Lindseth, A. A. *Schoolhouses, Courthouses, and Statehouses: Solving the Funding-Achievement Puzzle in America's Public Schools*. Princeton: Princeton University Press, 2009.

Hanushek, E. A., and Raymond, M. "Does School Accountability Lead to Improved School Performance?" *Journal of Policy Analysis and Management*, 24(2) (2005): 297–329.

Hanushek, E. A., and Rivkin, S. G. "School Quality and the Black-White Achievement Gap." *NBER Working Paper* (2006): #12651.

Hanushek, E. A., and Somers, J. A. "Schooling, Inequality, and the Impact of Government." In *The Causes and Consequences of Increasing Inequality*, edited by Finis Welch (pp. 169–99). Chicago: University of Chicago Press, 2001.

Harris, A. R., Evans, W. N., and Schwab, R. M. "Education Spending in an Aging America." *Journal of Public Economics*, 81 (2001): 449–72.

Hayes, K., and Chang, S. "The Relative Efficiency of City Manager and Mayor-Council Forms of Government." *Southern Economic Journal*, 57(1) (1990): 167–77.

Hedges, Larry V., and Greenwald, Rob. "Have Times Changed? The Relation between School Resources and Student Performance." In *Does Money Matter? The Effect of School Resources on Student Achievement and Adult Success*, edited by G. Burtless (pp. 74–92). Washington, DC: Brookings Institution, 1996.

Hedges, Larry V., Laine, Richard D., and Greenwald, R. "Does Money Matter? A Meta-Analysis of Studies of the Effects of Differential School Inputs on Student Outcomes." *Educational Researcher*, 23 (1994): 5–14.

Hertert, L., Busch, C., and Odden, A. "School Financing Inequities among the States: The Problem from a National Perspective." *Journal of Education Finance*, 19(3) (1994): 231–55.

Higgins, B., and Savoie, D. *Regional Development Theories and Their Application*. New Brunswick: Transaction Publishers, 1995.

Hirsch, B. T., and Macpherson, D. A. "Union Membership and Coverage Database from the Current Population Survey: Note." *Industrial and Labor Relations Review*, 56(2) (2003): 349–54.

Hirsch, B. T., and Schumacher, E. J. "Match Bias in Wage Gap Estimates Due to Earnings Imputation." *Journal of Labor Economics*, 22(3) (2004): 689–722.

Holzer, H. "The Spatial Mismatch Hypothesis: What has the Evidence Shown?" *Urban Studies*, 28 (1991): 105–22.

Horowitz, H. "Unseparate but Unequal: The Emerging Fourteenth Amendment Issue in Public School Education." *UCLA Law Review*, 13 (1966): 1147–72.

Howell, H. G. *Besieged: School Boards and the Future of Education Politics.* Washington, DC: The Brookings Institution, 2005.

Howell-Moroney, M. "The Tiebout Hypothesis 50 Years Later: Lessons and Lingering Challenges for Metropolitan Governance in the 21st Century." *Public Administration Review*, 68(1) (2008): 97–109.

Hoxby, C. "How Much Does School Spending Depend On Family Income? The Historical Origins of the Current School Finance Dilemma." *American Economic Review*, 88 (1998): 309–14.

Hoxby, Caroline M., and Gretchen Weingarth. *Taking race out of the equation: School reassignment and the structure of peer effects.* No. 7867. Working paper, 2005.

Hoxby, C. M. "Does Competition Among Public Schools Benefit Students and Taxpayers? Evidence from Natural Variation in School Districting." *NBER Working Paper* 1994: No. 4979.

Hoxby, C. M. "The Productivity of Schools and Other Local Public Goods Producers." *Journal of Public Economics*, 74 (1999): 1–30.

Hoxby, C. M. "Does Competition Among Public Schools Benefit Students and Taxpayers? Reply." *American Economic Review*, 97(5) (2007): 2038–55.

Hoxby, C. M. "Are Efficiency and Equity in School Finance Substitute or Complements?" *Journal of Economic Perspectives*, 10 (1996a): 51–72.

Hoxby, C. M. "How Teachers' Unions Affect Education Production." *The Quarterly Journal of Economics*, 111(3) (1996b): 671–718.

Hoxby, C. M. "Does Competition Among Public Schools Benefit Students and Taxpayers?" *American Economic Review*, 90(5) (2000): 1209–38.

Hughes, M. A. "Federal Roadblocks to Regional Cooperation." In *Urban- Suburban Interdependencies*, edited by R. Greenstein and W. Wiewel (pp. 161–80). Cambridge: The Lincoln Institute of Land Policy, 2000.

Ihlanfeldt, K. R., and Sjoquist, D. J. "The Spatial Mismatch Hypothesis: A Review of Recent Studies and Their Implications for Welfare Reform." *Housing Policy Debate*, 9 (1998): 849–92.

Imazeki, J., and Reschovsky, A. "Does No Child Left Behind Place a Fiscal Burden on States? Evidence from Texas." *Education Finance and Policy*, 1(2) (2006): 217–46.

Jackson, C. "Student Demographics, Teacher Sorting, and Teacher Quality: Evidence from the End of School Desegregation." *Journal of Labor Economics*, 27(2) (2009): 213–56.

Jargowsky, P. *Poverty and Place.* New York: Russell Sage Foundation, 1997.

Jimenez, B. S., and Hendrick, R. "Is Government Consolidation the Answer?" *State and Local Government Review*, 42(3) (2010): 258–70.

Jung, C. "Forms of Government and Spending on Common Municipal Functions: A Longitudinal Approach." *International Review of Administrative Sciences*, 72(3) (2006): 363–76.

Kain, J. "Housing Segregation, Negro Employment and Metropolitan Decentralization." *Quarterly Journal of Economics*, 82(2) (1968): 175–97.

Kenny, L. "Economies of Scale in Schooling." *Economics of Education Review*, 2 (1982): 1–24.

Kirp, D. L. "The Poor, the Schools, and Equal Protection." *Harvard Educational Review*, 38 (1968): 635–68.

Koretz, D., and Hamilton, L. "Testing for Accountability in K–12." In *Educational Measurement*, edited by R. L. Brennan (4th ed., pp. 531–78). Westport, CT: American Council on Education and Prayer, 2006.

Koski, W. S., and Hahnel, J. "The Past, Present and Possible Futures of Educational Finance Reform Litigation." In *Handbook of Research in Education Finance and Policy*, edited by H. F. Ladd and Edward B. Fiske (pp. 57–75). New York: Routledge, 2015.

Kozol, J. *Death at an Early Age*. Boston, MA: Houghton Mifflin, 1967.

Kozol, J. *Savage Inequalities: Children in America's Schools*. New York: Crown, 1992.

Kraft, M. E., and Furlong, S. R. *Public Policy: Politics, Analysis, and Alternatives* (3rd ed.). Washington, DC: Congressional Quarterly Press, 2017.

Ladd, H., and Zelli, F. "School-Based Accountability in North Carolina: The Responses of School Principals." *Education Administration Quarterly*, 38(4) (2002): 494–529.

Ladd, H., Chalk, R., and Hansen, J. *Equity and Adequacy in Education Finance: Issues and Perspectives*. Washington, DC: National Academy Press, 1999.

Lalvani, M. "Can Decentralization Limit Government Growth? A Test of the Leviathan Hypothesis for the Indian Federation." *Publius*, 32(5) (2002): 25–45.

Lee, J. *Tracking Achievement Gaps and Assessing the Impact of NCLB on the Gaps*. Cambridge, MA: Harvard Civil Rights Project, 2006.

LeRoux, K., Brandenburger, P. W., and Pandey, S. K. "Interlocal Service Cooperation in U.S. Cities: A Social Network Explanation." *Public Administration Review*, 70(2) (2010): 268–78.

Levin, H. M. "Issues in Education Privatization." In *Handbook of Research in Education Finance and Policy*, edited by H. F. Ladd and Edward B. Fiske (pp. 427–38). New York: Routledge, 2015.

Linn, R. L. "Assessment and Accountability." *Educational Researcher*, 29(2) (2000): 4–16.

Lowery, D. "A Transaction Costs Model of Metropolitan Governance: Allocation vs. Redistribution in Urban America." *Journal of Public Administration Research and Theory*, 10 (2000): 49–78.

Lowry, R. C. "Fiscal Policy in the American States, Chapter 10." In *Politics in the American States: A Comparative Analysis*, edited by V. Gray and R. L. Hanson (9th ed.). Washington, DC: CQ Press, 2008.

Lyons, W. "Reform and Response in American Cities: Structure and Policy Reconsidered." *Social Science Quarterly*, 59(1) (1978): 118–32.

Lyons, W., and Lowery, D. "Governmental Fragmentation Versus Consolidation: Five Public Choice Myths about How To Create Informed, Involved, and Happy Citizens." *Public Administration Review*, 49 (1989): 533–43.

MacDonald, L. "The Impact of Government Structure on Local Public Expenditures." *Public Choice*, 136(3–4) (2008): 457–73.

Marlow, M. L. "Public Education Supply and Student Performance." *Applied Economics*, 29 (1997): 617–26.

Marlow, M. L. "Spending, School Structure, and Public Education Quality: Evidence from California." *Economics of Education Review*, 19 (2000): 89–106.

McGinnis, M. D. (ed.). *Polycentricity and Local Public Economies: Readings from the Workshop in Political Theory and Policy Analysis*. Ann Arbor: University of Michigan Press, 1999.

McGuire, T. J., and Papke, L. E. "Local Funding of Schools: The Property Tax and Its Alternatives." In *Handbook of Research in Education Finance and Policy*, edited by H. F. Ladd and Edward B. Fiske (pp. 392–407). New York: Routledge, 2015.

Meier, K., Polinard, J., and Wrinkle, R. "Bureaucracy and Organizational Performance: Causality Arguments About Public Schools." *American Journal of Political Science*, 44(3) (2000): 590–602.

Merrifield, J. D. "The Institutional and Political Factors Which Influence Taxation." *Public Choice*, 69 (1991): 295–310.

Merrifield, J. D. "State Government Expenditure Determinants and Tax Revenue Determinants Revisited." *Public Choice*, 102(1/2) (2000): 25–50.

Mickelson, R. A. "Achieving the Educational Opportunity in the Wake of the Judicial Retreat from Race Sensitive Remedies: Lessons from North Carolina." *American University Law Review*, 52(6) (2003): 1477–506.

Mickelson, R. "Subverting Swann: First-and Second-Generation Segregation in the Charlotte Mecklenburg Schools." *American Educational Research Journal*, 38(2) (2001): 215–52.

Miller, D. *The Regional Governing of Metropolitan America*. Boulder, CO: Westview Press, 2002.

Millimet, D. L., and Collier, T. "Efficiency in Public Schools: Does Competition Matter?" *Journal of Econometrics*, 145(1–2) (2008): 134–57.

Millimet, D. L., and Rangaprasad, V. "Strategic Competition amongst Public Schools." *Regional Science & Urban Economics*, 37(2) (2007): 199–219.

Minorini, P. A., and Sugarman, S. D. "School Finance Litigation in the Name of Educational Equity: Its Evolution, Impact and Future." In *Equity and Adequacy in Education Finance: Issues and Perspectives*, edited by H. F. Ladd, R. Chalk, and J. S. Hansen (pp. 34–71). Washington, DC: National Academy Press, 1999.

Moe, T. (ed.). *A Primer on America's Schools*. Stanford, CA: Hoover Institution Press, 2001.

Morgan, D. R., and Mareschal, P. "Central-City/Suburban Inequality and Metropolitan Political Fragmentation." *Urban Affairs Review*, 34 (1999): 578–95.

Murnane, R., Willet, J., Bub, K., and McCartney, K. "Understanding Trends in the Black-White Achievement Gap during the First Years of School." *Brookings-Wharton Papers on Urban Affairs* (2006): 97–127.

Murray, S., Evans, W., and Schwab, R. "Education-Finance Reform and the Distribution of Education Resources." *American Economic Review*, 88(4) (1998): 789–812.

Musgrave, R. A. "The Voluntary Exchange Theory of Public Economy." *Quarterly Journal of Economics*, 52 (1939): 213–17.

Nelson, M. A. "An Empirical Analysis of State and Local Tax Structure in the Context of the Leviathan Model of Government." *Public Choice*, 49(3) (1986): 283–94.

Niskanen, W. A. *Bureaucracy and Representative Government.* Chicago: Aldine, Atherton, 1971.

Nye, B., Hedges, L. V., and Konstantopoulos, S. "The Long-Term Effects of Small Classes: A Five-Year Follow-Up of the Tennessee Class Size Experiment." *Educational Evaluation and Policy Analysis*, 21 (1999): 127–43.

Nye, B., Konstantopoulas, S., and Hedges, L. "How Large Are Teacher Effects?" *Educational Evaluation and Policy Analysis*, 26(3) (2004): 237–57.

Oakes, J. *Keeping Track: How Schools Structure Inequality.* New Haven, CT: Yale University Press, 1985.

Oakes, J. *Multiplying Inequalities: The Effects of Race, Social Class, and Tracking On Opportunities To Learn Mathematics and Science.* Santa Monica, CA: RAND, 1990.

Oakerson, R. *Governing Local Public Economies: Creating the Civic Metropolis.* Oakland, CA: Institute of Contemporary Studies Press, 1999.

Oakerson, Ronald J. *The Organization of Local Public Economies: A Commission Report.* Advisory Commission on Intergovernmental Relations, 1987 (ACIR, 1987).

Oates, W. E. "Searching for Leviathan: An Empirical Study." *American Economic Review*, 75(4) (1985): 748–57.

Odden, A. R., and Picus, L. O. *School Finance: A Policy Perspective.* Boston: McGraw-Hill, 2000.

Odden, A. R., and Picus, L. O. *School Finance: A Policy Perspective.* Boston: McGraw-Hill, 2013.

Orfield, G., and Yun, J. *Resegregation in American Schools.* Cambridge, MA: Harvard Civil Rights Project, 1999.

Ostrom, E. *The Delivery of Urban Services.* Beverly Hills, CA: Sage, 1976.

Ostrom, E., and Smith, D. "On the Fate of 'Lilliputs' in Metropolitan Policing." *Public Administration Review*, 36 (1976): 192–99.

Ostrom, E., Parks, R. B., and Whitaker, G. P. *Patterns of Metropolitan Policing.* Cambridge, MA: Ballinger Publishing Company, 1978.

Ostrom, V. *The Meaning of Democracy and the Vulnerability of Democracy.* Ann Arbor: University of Michigan Press, 1997.

Ostrom, V., Tiebout, C. M., and Warren, R. "The Organization of Government in Metropolitan Areas: A Theoretical Inquiry." *American Political Science Review*, 55(4) (1961): 831–42.

Parks, R. B., and Oakerson, R. J. "Comparative Metropolitan Organization: Service Production and Governance Structures in St. Louis (MO) and Allegheny County (PA)." *Publius*, 23(1) (1993): 19–39.

Parks, R. B., and Oakerson, R. J. "Regionalism, Localism and Metropolitan Governance: Suggestions from the Research Program on Local Public Economics." *State and Local Government Review*, 32(3) (2000): 169–79.

Peltzman, S. "The Political Economy of the Decline of American Public Education." *Journal of Law and Economics*, 36(1) (1993): 331–70.

Peltzman, S. "The Political Economy of Public Education: Non-College Bound Students." *Journal of Law and Economics*, 39(1) (1996): 73–120.

Persson, Torsten, and Tabellini, Guido. *The Economic Effects of Constitutions.* Cambridge, MA: MIT Press, 2003.

Peterson, P. *City Limits*. Chicago: University of Chicago Press, 1981.

Peterson, P. E. *Saving Schools: From Horace Mann to Virtual Learning.* Cambridge: The Belknap Press of Harvard University Press, 2010.

Picus, L. O., Goertz, M., and Odden, A. "Intergovermental Aid Formulas and Case Studies." In *Handbook of Research in Education Finance and Policy*, edited by H. F. Ladd and Edward B. Fiske (pp. 295–312). New York: Routledge, 2015.

Podgrusky, M. J. "Is Teacher Pay Adequate?" In *School Money Trials: The Legal Pursuit of Educational Adequacy*, edited by Martin R. West and Paul E. Peterson (pp. 131–55). Washington, DC: Brookings Institution Press, 2007.

Poterba, J. "State Response to Fiscal Crises: The Effects of Budgetary Institutions and Politics." *Journal of Political Economy*, 102 (1994): 799–821.

Poterba, J. "Budget Institutions and Fiscal Policy in the U.S. States." *American Economic Review*, 86 (1996): 395–400.

Poterba, J. M. "Demographic Structure and the Political Economy of Public Education." *Journal of Policy Analysis and Management*, 16(1) (1997): 48–66.

Preston, V., and McLafferty, S. "Spatial Mismatch Research in the 1990s: Progress and Potential." *Papers in Regional Science*, 78 (1999): 387–402.

Raphael, S., and Stoll, M. A. "Job Sprawl and the Suburbanization of Poverty." *Brookings Metropolitan Policy Program* (2010): 1–20.

Reardon, S. F. *Thirteen Ways of Looking at the Black-White Test Score Gap*. Stanford University Mimeograph, 2007.

Rivkin, S. G., Hanushek, E. A., and Kain, J. F. "Teachers, Schools, and Academic Achievement." *Working Paper #6691*, National Bureau of Economic Research, 1998.

Rodden, J. "Reviving Leviathan: Fiscal Federalism and the Growth of Government." *International Organization*, 57(4) (2003): 695–729.

Roscigno, Vincent J., Tomaskovic-Devey, Donald, and Crowley, Martha. "Education and the Inequalities of Place." *Social Forces*, 84(4) (2006): 2121–45.

Rothstein, J. "Does Competition Among Public Schools Benefit Students and Taxpayers? A Comment on Hoxby (2000)." *NBER Working Paper* (2005): #11215.

Rothstein, J. "Does Competition Among Public Schools Benefit Students and Taxpayers? Comment." *American Economic Review*, 97(5) (2007): 2026–37.

Rothstein, R. *Class and Schools: Using Social, Economic, and Educational Reform to Close the Black-White Achievement Gap*. Economic Policy Institute; Columbia University, 2004.

Rothstein, R. "Fact-Challenged Policy." *Policy Memorandum# 182*. Economic Policy Institute, 2011.

Roza, Marguerite. *Educational Economics: Where Do School Funds Go?* Washington, DC: Urban Institute Press, 2010.

Rubinfeld, D., Shapiro, P., and Roberts, J. "Tiebout Bias and the Demand for Local Public Schooling." *Review of Economic and Statistics*, 69(3) (1987): 426–37.

Rusk, D. *Cities without Suburbs*. Washington, DC: Woodrow Wilson Press, 1993.

Ryan, J. E., and Saunders, T. "Foreword to Symposium on School Finance Litigation: Emerging Trends or New Dead Ends?" *Yale Law & Policy Review*, 22(2) (2004): 463–80.

Saha, S. "City-Level Analysis of the Effect of Political Regimes on Public Good Provision." *Public Choice*, 147(1–2) (2011): 155–71.

Samuelson, P. A. "The Pure Theory of Public Expenditures." *Review of Economics and Statistics*, 36(4) (1954): 387–89.

Sanders, W. L. "Value Added Assessment." *The School Administrator*, 55(11) (1998): 24–32.

Santerre, R. E. "Leviathan or Median Voter: Who Runs City Hall?" *Eastern Economic Journal*, 17(1) (1991): 5–14.

Schneider, M. "Fragmentation and the Growth of Local Government." *Public Choice*, 48 (1986): 255.

Schneider, M. *The Competitive City: The Political Economy of Suburbia*. Pittsburgh, PA: University of Pittsburgh Press, 1989.

Schneider, M., Teske, P., Roch, C., and Marschall, M. "Network to Nowhere: Segregation and Stratification in Networks of Information about Schools." *American Journal of Political Science*, 41 (1997): 1201–23.

Slagle, M. "A Comparison of Spatial Statistical Methods in a School Finance Policy Context." *Journal of Education Finance*, 35(3) (2010): 199–216.

Springer, M. G., Houck, E. A., and Guthrie, J. W. "History and Scholarship Regarding United States Education Finance and Policy." In *Handbook of Research in Education Finance and Policy*, edited by H. F. Ladd and Edward B. Fiske (pp. 3–22). New York: Routledge, 2008.

Springer, M. G., Houck, E. A., and Guthrie, J. W. "History and Scholarship Regarding United States Education Finance and Policy." In *Handbook of Research in Education Finance and Policy*, edited by H. F. Ladd and Edward B. Fiske (pp. 25–44). New York: Routledge, 2015.

Squires, Gregory D. "Urban Sprawl and the Uneven Development of Metropolitan America." In *Urban Sprawl: Causes, Consequences and Policy Responses*, edited by Gregory D. Squires (pp. 1–22). Washington, DC: Urban Institute Press, 2002.

Stansel, D. "Interjurisdictional Competition and Local Government Spending in U.S. Metropolitan Areas." *Public Finance Review*, 34 (2006): 173–94.

Stecher, B., Barron, S., Chun, T., and Ross, T. *The Effects of the Washington State Education Reform on Schools and Classrooms.* Los Angeles: Center for Research on Evaluation, Standards and Student Testing, 2000.

Stephens, G. R., and Wikstrom, N. *Metropolitan Government and Governance: Theoretical Perspectives, Empirical Analysis, and the Future.* New York: Oxford University Press, 2000.

Stone, D. *Policy Paradox: The Art of Political Decision Making.* New York: W.W. Norton, 2002.

Strang, D. "The Administrative Transformation of American Education: School District Consolidation, 1938–1980." *Administrative Science Quarterly*, 23(3) (1987): 352–66.

Stumm, T. J., and Corrigan, M. T. "City Managers: Do They Promote Fiscal Efficiency?" *Journal of Urban Affairs*, 20(3) (1998): 343–51.

Summers, A. "Regionalization Efforts Between Big Cities and Their Suburbs." In *Urban- Suburban Interdependencies*, edited by R. Greenstein and W. Wiewel (pp. 181–93). Cambridge: The Lincoln Institute of Land Policy, 2000.

Tiebout, Charles. "A Pure Theory of Local Expenditure." *Journal of Political Economy*, 64 (1956, October): 416–24.

U.S. Census Bureau, Census of Governments. *Survey of Local Government Finances – School Systems.* Washington, DC: U.S. Dept. of Education, National Center for Education Statistics, 2007.

U.S. Department of Education, National Center for Education Statistics. *Digest of Education Statistics, 2011* (NCES 2012-001). Washington, DC: U.S. Dept. of Education, National Center for Education Statistics, 2012.

U.S. Dept. of Education, National Center for Education Statistics. *Common Core of Data: Public School Districts, 1980–1981 [Computer file]. ICPSR Version.* Washington, DC: U.S. Dept. of Education, National Center for Education Statistics [producer], 1981. Ann Arbor, MI: Inter- university Consortium for Political and Social Research [distributor], 1999. doi:10.3886/ICPSR02132.v1.

U.S. Dept. of Education, National Center for Education Statistics. *Common Core of Data: Public School Districts, 1981–1982 [Computer file]. ICPSR Version.* Washington, DC: U.S. Dept. of Education, National Center for Education Statistics [producer], 1982. Ann Arbor, MI: Inter- university Consortium for Political and Social Research [distributor], 1999. doi:10.3886/ICPSR02133.v1.

U.S. Dept. of Education, National Center for Education Statistics. *Common Core of Data: Public School Districts, 1982–1983 [Computer file]. ICPSR Version.* Washington, DC: U.S. Dept. of Education, National Center for Education Statistics [producer], 1983. Ann Arbor, MI: Inter- university Consortium for Political and Social Research [distributor], 1999. doi:10.3886/ICPSR02134.v1.

Voith, R. "Do Suburbs Need Cities?" *Journal of Regional Science*, 38(3) (1998): 445–64.

Wayne, A. J., and Youngs, P. "Teacher Characteristics and Student Achievement Gains: A Review." *Review of Educational Research*, 73 (2003): 89–122.

Weiher, G. R. *The Fractured Metropolis: Political Fragmentation and Metropolitan Segregation.* Albany, NY: SUNY Press, 1991.

Wenglinsky, Harold. "How Money Matters: The Effect of School District Spending on Academic Achievement." *Sociology of Education*, 70(3) (1997): 221–37.

Wells, A. S. *Time to Choose: American at the Crossroads of School Choice Policy*. New York: Hill and Wang, 1993.

West, Martin R., and Peterson, Paul E. *School Money Trials: The Legal Pursuit of Educational Adequacy*. Washington, DC: Brookings Institution Press, 2007.

Williams, P. K., McLaughlin, D., Glander, M. C., and Fowler, W. J. Jr. *Documentation of the NCES Longitudinal School District Fiscal-Nonfiscal Detail File, Fiscal Years 1990 to 2002* (NCES 2006-320). U.S. Department of Education. Washington, DC: National Center for Education Statistics, 2006.

Wilson, W. J. *The Truly Disadvantaged: The Inner City, The Underclass and Public Policy*. Chicago, L.: University of Chicago Press, 1987.

Wilson, W. J. "The Role of the Environment in the Black-White Test Score Gap." In *The Black-White Test Score Gap*, edited by C. Jencks and M. Phillips (pp. 501–10). Washington, DC: Brookings Institution Press, 1998.

Wilson, Kathryn S., Lambright, Kristina T., and Smeeding, Timothy M. "School Finance and Equality of Opportunity: Equal Dollars or Equal Chances for Success?" *Education Finance and Policy*, 1(4) (2006): 396–424.

Wise, A. *Rich Schools, Poor Schools: The Promise of Equal Opportunity*. Chicago, IL: University of Chicago Press, 1968.

Woessmann, L., and Peterson, P. E. (eds.). *Schools and the Equal Opportunity Problem*. Cambridge, MA: MIT Press, 2007.

Wolfe, A. *School Choice. The Moral Debate*. Princeton, NJ: Princeton University Press, 2003.

Wong, K. K. *Funding Public Schools: Politics and Policies*. Lawrence: University Press of Kansas, 1999.

Wood, C. "Scope and Patterns of Metropolitan Governance in Urban America: Probing the Complexities in the Kansas City Region." *American Review of Public Administration*, 36(3) (2005): 337–53.

Wooldridge, J. *Introductory Econometrics–A Modern Approach*. Thomson-South Western, 2006.

Yeung, R. "The Effects of Fiscal Decentralization on the Size of Government: A Meta-Analysis." *Public Budgeting and Finance*, 29(4) (2009): 1–23.

Yeung, Wei-Jun Jean, and Pfeiffer, K. M. "The Black-White Test Score Gap and Early Home Environment." *Social Science Research*, 38 (2009): 412–37.

Zanzig, B. R. "Measuring the Impact of Competition in Local Government Education Markets on the Cognitive Achievement of Students." *Economics of Education Review*, 16 (1997): 431–41.

Zax, J. S. "Is There a Leviathan in Your Neighborhood?" *American Economic Review*, 79(3) (1989): 560–67.

Index

About the Author

Nandan K. Jha is an assistant professor in the Department of Political Science at Valdosta State University. He teaches courses in public policy and public administration. His research broadly focuses on K-16 education policy and local governments in the United States. He uses quantitative research designs to study issues pertaining to the structural and institutional inequity problems in the regional context of the education policy area. His research on interjurisdictional competition and type of political institutions in local governments and inequity and effectiveness in K-12 public education exemplifies this line of research. His research also focuses on how comparative socio-politico-economic-racial backgrounds are related with student's higher educational outcomes. He has published articles and books in *American Educational Research Journal*, *Social Science Research*, *Research in Higher Education*, and Sage Publications. He is currently studying the implications of inequity in socioeconomic opportunity structure of place on student educational outcomes.

www.ingramcontent.com/pod-product-compliance
Lightning Source LLC
Chambersburg PA
CBHW022325280326
41932CB00010B/1227